NEWPORT

A HISTORY AND CELEBRATION
OF THE CITY

BOB TRETT

Produced by The Francis Frith Collection
exclusively for

OTTAKAR'S

www.ottakars.co.uk

First published in the United Kingdom in 2004 by
Frith Book Company Ltd

Hardback Edition 2004
ISBN 1-90493-839-6

British Library Cataloguing in Publication Data

Newport - A History and Celebration of the City
Bob Trett

Frith Book Company Ltd
Frith's Barn, Teffont,
Salisbury, Wiltshire SP3 5QP
Tel: +44 (0) 1722 716 376
Email: info@francisfrith.co.uk
www.francisfrith.co.uk

Printed and bound in Italy

Front Cover: **NEWPORT, COMMERCIAL STREET 1901** 47896t

Additional photographs by Bob Trett
Domesday extract used in timeline by kind permission of
Alecto Historical Editions, www.domesdaybook.org.
Aerial photographs reproduced under licence from
Simmons Aerofilms Limited.
Historical Ordnance Survey maps reproduced under licence from
Homecheck.co.uk
Other illustrations produced courtesy of www.newportpast.com

*The colour-tinting in this book is for illustrative purposes only,
and is not intended to be historically accurate*

Contents

NEWPORT FROM THE AIR 1929 AF29304

Historical Timeline for Newport

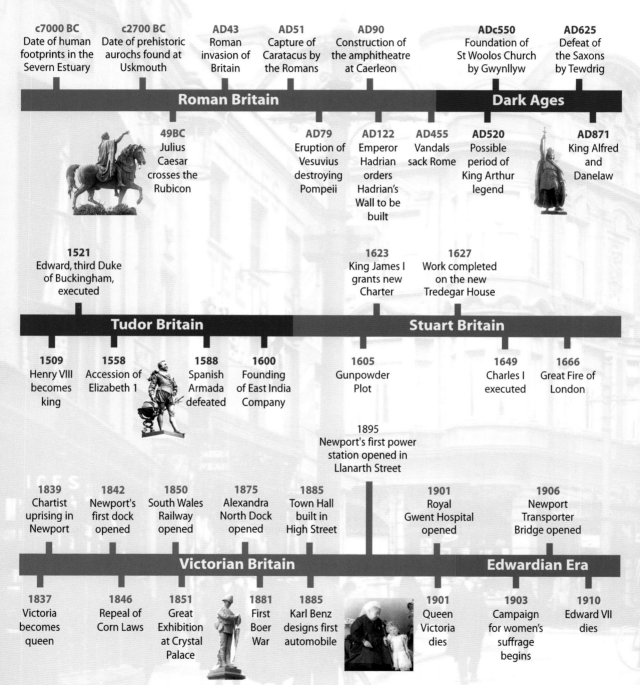

c7000 BC
Date of human footprints in the Severn Estuary

c2700 BC
Date of prehistoric aurochs found at Uskmouth

AD43
Roman invasion of Britain

AD51
Capture of Caratacus by the Romans

AD90
Construction of the amphitheatre at Caerleon

ADc550
Foundation of St Woolos Church by Gwynllyw

AD625
Defeat of the Saxons by Tewdrig

Roman Britain

Dark Ages

49BC
Julius Caesar crosses the Rubicon

AD79
Eruption of Vesuvius destroying Pompeii

AD122
Emperor Hadrian orders Hadrian's Wall to be built

AD455
Vandals sack Rome

AD520
Possible period of King Arthur legend

AD871
King Alfred and Danelaw

1521
Edward, third Duke of Buckingham, executed

1623
King James I grants new Charter

1627
Work completed on the new Tredegar House

Tudor Britain

Stuart Britain

1509
Henry VIII becomes king

1558
Accession of Elizabeth 1

1588
Spanish Armada defeated

1600
Founding of East India Company

1605
Gunpowder Plot

1649
Charles I executed

1666
Great Fire of London

1895
Newport's first power station opened in Llanarth Street

1839
Chartist uprising in Newport

1842
Newport's first dock opened

1850
South Wales Railway opened

1875
Alexandra North Dock opened

1885
Town Hall built in High Street

1901
Royal Gwent Hospital opened

1906
Newport Transporter Bridge opened

Victorian Britain

Edwardian Era

1837
Victoria becomes queen

1846
Repeal of Corn Laws

1851
Great Exhibition at Crystal Palace

1881
First Boer War

1885
Karl Benz designs first automobile

1901
Queen Victoria dies

1903
Campaign for women's suffrage begins

1910
Edward VII dies

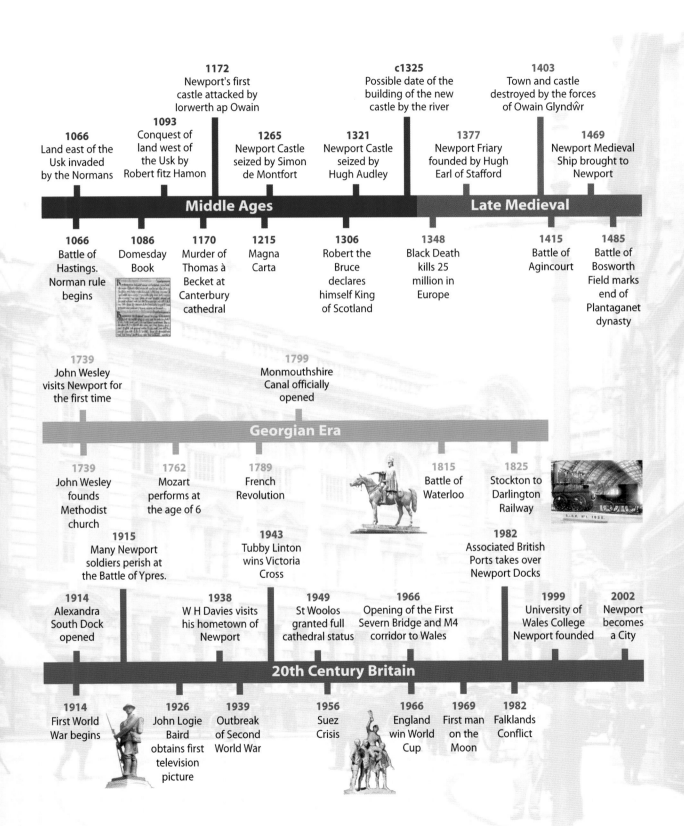

1066 Land east of the Usk invaded by the Normans

1093 Conquest of land west of the Usk by Robert fitz Hamon

1172 Newport's first castle attacked by Iorwerth ap Owain

1265 Newport Castle seized by Simon de Montfort

1321 Newport Castle seized by Hugh Audley

c1325 Possible date of the building of the new castle by the river

1377 Newport Friary founded by Hugh Earl of Stafford

1403 Town and castle destroyed by the forces of Owain Glyndŵr

1469 Newport Medieval Ship brought to Newport

Middle Ages   Late Medieval

1066 Battle of Hastings. Norman rule begins

1086 Domesday Book

1170 Murder of Thomas à Becket at Canterbury cathedral

1215 Magna Carta

1306 Robert the Bruce declares himself King of Scotland

1348 Black Death kills 25 million in Europe

1415 Battle of Agincourt

1485 Battle of Bosworth Field marks end of Plantaganet dynasty

1739 John Wesley visits Newport for the first time

1799 Monmouthshire Canal officially opened

Georgian Era

1739 John Wesley founds Methodist church

1762 Mozart performs at the age of 6

1789 French Revolution

1815 Battle of Waterloo

1825 Stockton to Darlington Railway

1915 Many Newport soldiers perish at the Battle of Ypres.

1943 Tubby Linton wins Victoria Cross

1982 Associated British Ports takes over Newport Docks

1914 Alexandra South Dock opened

1938 W H Davies visits his hometown of Newport

1949 St Woolos granted full cathedral status

1966 Opening of the First Severn Bridge and M4 corridor to Wales

1999 University of Wales College Newport founded

2002 Newport becomes a City

20th Century Britain

1914 First World War begins

1926 John Logie Baird obtains first television picture

1939 Outbreak of Second World War

1956 Suez Crisis

1966 England win World Cup

1969 First man on the Moon

1982 Falklands Conflict

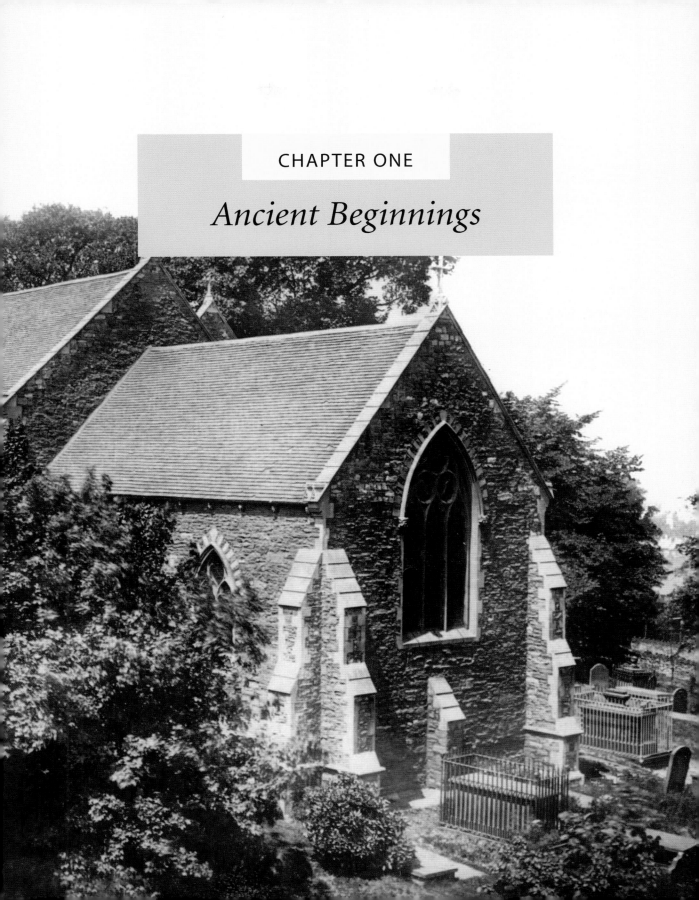

CHAPTER ONE

Ancient Beginnings

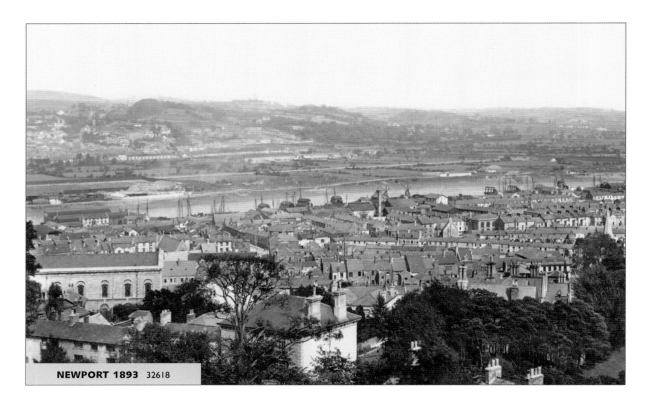

NEWPORT 1893 32618

NEWPORT STANDS at a crossing point. Lying in the south-east corner of Wales, it is a border city where English and Welsh influences intermingle. For much of its history Newport was a marcher lordship, with control resting in the hands of powerful barons who enjoyed many privileges and considerable independence from the English crown.

Geographically, Newport lies between the uplands of the Welsh mining valleys to the north-west, the Black Mountains to the north, the rolling hills of Monmouthshire to the north-east and the lowland area of the Severn Valley to the south. The city stretches either side of the River Usk, a few miles from where the mouth of the river joins the Severn Estuary. Newport's bridges take traffic over the Usk, the first great obstacle to entry from England into South Wales after crossing the Wye or the Severn.

The great Severn estuary, together with its tributary rivers, has the second highest tidal range in the world. The difference between high water and low water can be nearly 15 metres. Thus at low tide vast expanses of mud are exposed. The flat lands to the south of Newport are known as the Gwent Levels and stretch from Chepstow in the east to Rumney in the west. This area is low-lying and needs sea walls for coastal protection. Ever since the Roman period vast areas of the original marshland have been drained for use in farming.

THE BRIDGE AND THE CASTLE 1896 38698

Floods

The area around Newport has always been prone to flooding, and even the sea walls and embankments have at times failed to keep the water out. The combination of high tides, floodwater surging down the Usk from the Brecon Beacons, and wind direction can cause exceptional rises in the river levels. Excavations in the Gwent Levels and the Severn Estuary revealed a series of layers of tidal mud burying prehistoric woodland and fenland. In later times, Goldcliff Priory was flooded and partly destroyed in 1424, Duffryn was flooded in 1466 when the River Ebbw, flowing into the Usk, topped its banks, and in 1606-67 there was a great flood that drowned around 2,000 people in 26 parishes. This flood is commemorated in wall plaques of the churches at Goldcliff, Peterstone, Redwick and St Brides, marking the height that the waters reached.

Who were the earliest inhabitants of Newport? In 1908 a number of human skulls and other bones were found in what had been a limestone cave at Ifton, east of Newport. Quarrying had destroyed the cave, but it is possible that these bones may be some of the earliest human remains from South Wales. They had been deliberately interred and arranged on a ledge in the cave. Often it is possible to date early bones using a technique called radiocarbon dating, and recently dates of around 2,160BC and 2,400BC have been made on the Ifton bones.

Long before the town was built, human beings wandered near the mouth of the River Usk. These were nomadic people hunting for wild pigs and deer, and trapping fish in the creeks of the Severn Estuary. The most sensational evidence for their existence came in 1989, when local archaeologist Derek Upton spotted tracks of human footprints in the tidal mud at Nash to the south of the present city. Nothing unusual in normal circumstances maybe - but these disappeared underneath layers of peat that were up to 7,000 years old. The footprints had to be older than the peat and this made them amongst the oldest footprints found in Britain. More and more evidence has now come to light from various places on the foreshore, including burnt bone and flint tools from nearby Goldcliff, and the enormous bones of wild cattle known as aurochsen. These beasts could be as tall as two metres at the shoulder and had huge horns. An almost complete skeleton was discovered near Nash and is now on display in Newport Museum. This was dated to around 2,700 BC, towards the end of the Neolithic or New Stone Age, but is not as old as the human footprints found in the same area.

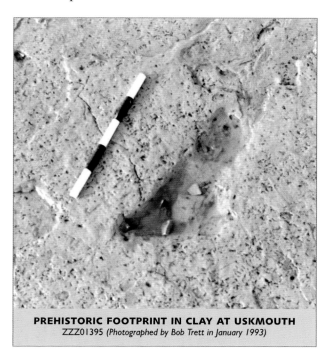

PREHISTORIC FOOTPRINT IN CLAY AT USKMOUTH
ZZZ01395 (Photographed by Bob Trett in January 1993)

Many other early bones have been discovered in the Newport area. In 1910 workmen excavating an extension to the Newport Docks found a human skull, as well as remains of early cattle, horse, sheep, wild pig and wolf. Archaeologists have managed to date the skull to about 2,000 BC. At this time people were still using stone tools, but had learnt to settle in one place and grow crops. In 1961 another skull was found near the River Usk, at the Orb Steelworks. This was embedded in clay and was found to date to about the time of Christ, probably just before the Romans came to Britain.

The earliest surviving prehistoric monument in Newport is a group of stones known as Gwern-y-Cleppa. The monument is just visible from the M4 motorway to the west of Newport, and was once a burial chamber, probably dating to between 2,000 and 4,000 BC. However by far the largest prehistoric monuments around Newport are the hill forts, mostly dating to the Iron Age, before the Roman conquest of Wales. The most impressive of these hill forts is the Gaer, also known as Tredegar Camp, which has a series of banks and ditches and overlooks the surrounding area. Even more spectacular is Twmbarlwm in Risca. On the top of this mountain is a hill fort overlooking the area for miles and visible from most of Newport.

There are at least 43 hillforts scattered around Newport and the former county of Gwent. But who built them? Legend suggests one explanation. In the 12th century a cleric called Geoffrey of Monmouth wrote a book called the 'History of the Kings of Britain'.

RISCA NEAR NEWPORT c1955 R328035

In the background is Twmbarlwm.

THE RAMPARTS OF THE GAER HILL FORT 2004 N25701k *(Bob Trett)*

Twmbarlwm can be seen in the background.

Geoffrey had a vivid imagination and recounted many of the myths and legends he had heard. In his 'History' he talks about two brothers, Belinus and Brennius, who were kings of Britain. The brothers fought a great number of battles with each other, but were eventually reconciled and decided to lead a joint army to attack Gaul (present day France). After they had captured Gaul they attacked and sacked the city of Rome in about 390 BC. Belinus then returned to Britain. Geoffrey says:

'He founded a certain city on the bank of the River Usk, near to the Severn Sea: this was the capital of Demetia and for a long time was called Kaerusc. When the Romans came the earlier name was dropped and it was re-named the City of the Legions, taking its title from the Roman legions that used to winter there'.

This is an obvious reference to Caerleon, the site of the Roman Legionary fortress, four miles to the north of the centre of Newport. But the fortress at Caerleon is much too late in date for a city founded by Belinus. Also the local tribe were called the Silures, not the Demetae who inhabited the area around modern Pembrokeshire. However above Caerleon is a hill fort known as Lodge Hill, surrounded by a series of ditches. An earlier name for this hill fort was Belinstock (or the stockade of Belin). Did the name come about because of the legend or was the site named

after a real person?

In the summer of 2000 the University of Wales College, Newport, carried out an excavation and found small structures, including an iron brooch and fragments of pottery dating to the middle of the Iron Age. It was certainly of a suitable date for Belinus, but hardly a suitable tribute to a King of Britain who had conquered Rome.

More is known about the local people of the Iron Age from Roman writers. Tacitus, in his history of the Roman commander Agricola, talks about the Silures:

'The swarthy faces of the Silures, the tendency of their hair to curl and the fact that Spain lies opposite, all lead one to believe that Spaniards crossed in ancient times and occupied the land'.

In another account by Tacitus, the 'Annals', he also tells us that the Silures put up some of the most serious resistance to the Roman invasion of their territory:

A RECONSTRUCTION OF AN IRON AGE ROUNDHOUSE ZZZ01297
(Reproduced by kind permission of the Ancient Technology Centre, Cranborne, Dorset)

'Then the Silures were attacked. Besides their own high courage, they put their trust in Caratacus, whose many battles, some doubtful, some victorious, had raised him to a pre-eminence among the princes of Britain'.

Caratacus was a prince of the Catuvellauni, a tribe in south-east Britain, who had been defeated during the Roman invasion of AD43. He fled to the west and by AD50 he was leading the Silures in their resistance. Eventually defeated, he fled to the north, but was handed over to the Romans in AD51. Caratacus has passed into Welsh legend and is commemorated in Welsh by the name Caradoc, also used by later Welsh princes. Nevertheless, the Silures continued to be a thorn in the side of the Romans and it is likely than many of the Newport hill forts would have seen fierce fighting.

Tacitus tells some more of the Silures' successes against the Romans:

'Whether it was that the removal of Caratacus led to carelessness in our military operations, as though the war was over, or that compassion for their great king's fate had whetted the enemy's appetite for vengeance, they surrounded a Prefect of the camp, with the legionary cohorts, which had been left behind to construct defences in the Silurian country; and had not help been quickly sent up to the besieged men from the neighbouring forts on receipt of the news, they would have been cut off to a man. As it was, the Prefect himself was killed, together with eight centurions and the bravest of the private soldiers'.

The Prefect was a senior professional soldier in a Roman legion, so this was a major disaster. There were other setbacks, but in the end their superior military might succeeded and by AD75 the Romans were able to build their large legionary fortress at Caerleon.

They called it Isca, probably after the name of the River Usk. Isca is now within the boundaries of the modern Newport, but Caerleon has its own history and was a separate town until 1974. However, during the Roman period the area for miles around may have been under the control of the legion based at Isca, which was called the Second Augustan Legion. This was a force of about 5,500 men, and its name is seen on many inscriptions found in the area. The legion was named after the Emperor Augustus, and was one of four that took part in the original invasion of Britain.

CAERLEON AMPHITHEATRE, ROMAN MILTARY RE-ENACTMENT 2004 N25716k *(Bob Trett)*

Roman Names

The names of Roman towns, fortresses and roads often cause of confusion. Many writers refer to the Roman fortress at Caerleon as Isca Silurum. This is incorrect. The Roman town at Caerwent was Venta Silurum (market town of the Silures) and Caerleon was just Isca. The most important surviving Roman document refers to Iscae Leg ii Aug (Isca of the Second Augustan Legion). This document is called the Antonine Itinerary and dates from the 2nd or 3rd

STAMP MARK FROM A TILE MADE BY THE SECOND AUGUSTAN LEGION AT CAERLEON
ZZZ01402

centuries AD. Antiquarians such as William Coxe, who wrote 'An Historical Tour in Monmouthshire' in 1801, have helped to perpetuate the wrong name. Similarly the name Via Julia for the main Roman road passing through the area is a later invention, not used by the Romans.

ARTIST'S IMPRESSION OF A ROMAN HELMET FOUND IN GERMANY
ZZZ01293

Isca was one of three permanent legionary fartresses in Britain and was occupied by the Second Augustan Legion until the end of the 3rd century. Even today the fortress remains are impressive and many of the finds from its excavations are now on display to the public in the Roman Legionary Museum in Caerleon. Scattered around Caerleon is more evidence of the Roman occupation. Outside the fortress itself was a large civilian settlement, and nearby are cemeteries where the names of many of the soldiers have been found on tombstones. There is less evidence of Roman activity in the area that was to become the later town of

Newport. A Roman villa is known to have existed to the east of the town. A stone coffin containing a skeleton was unearthed in 1939 at a limestone quarry in Lliswerry. Roman coins, brooches and other items have also been found and a considerable amount of Roman pottery from an area around Traston Road, Newport. The main civilian settlement was at Caerwent, known as Venta Silurum: the Silures had their own council to administer their affairs, and this was based at Caerwent.

The tidal areas of the foreshore of the Severn have produced extensive amounts of Roman material. Amongst the most interesting was a stone slab with an inscription. It was found in 1878, having been washed out by the tide below the sea wall at Goldcliff Pill. This may have been a boundary marker and refers to work done by the century (that is a military unit) of Statorius Maximus. Interestingly, work done on the other side of Newport, to the west, has provided evidence that the Romans were also digging drainage ditches on the low-lying land along the Severn. It is possible that Statorius Maximus may have been involved in this work, although the exact reason for the Goldcliff stone remains unknown.

A Roman road system existed to the north of Newport, connecting the Roman town of Caerwent (Venta Silurum) to the east, with Caerleon, and then continuing to the west towards Cardiff and north to the village of Bulmore and on to Usk. The only known Roman quays on the River Usk were found in 1968, to the south of the Roman fortress at Caerleon. These were built of stone and timber, and show the river had a different course in the Roman period, being much closer to the south of the fortress.

However Newport does lay claim to the most complete boat of the Roman period ever to have been found in Britain. In 1993 the remains of a small jetty or similar structure on the side of a filled-in creek were found at Barlands Farm, Magor. Next to this structure was a flat-bottomed boat some 9.5 metres long. The stern had been deliberately cut away but the bow of the boat and much of the hull survived. A small mast step showed that it originally had a sail. It is thought to have been a small coastal trading vessel, probably transporting a wide variety of goods around the Severn Estuary. Two coins found during the excavation were dated to the late 3rd century AD, and tree ring examination

showed that the wood used in constructing the boat had come from trees cut down between AD283 and AD326. Although the boat was of the Roman period, the structure of the vessel shows it was a native vessel and not a typical Roman boat. Following the excavation and dismantling of the boat the timbers were taken away for conservation. At present they are in store in Newport Museum awaiting a suitable place for them to be reassembled for display.

A full account of Caerleon is outside the scope of this book. Even so no account of the Newport area would be complete without some reference to its Roman remains. The most impressive of these is the amphitheatre. Built in about AD90, just outside the fortress walls, it is the only fully excavated amphitheatre to be seen in Britain. It could seat around 6,000 people, so would have been able to accommodate the whole legion if necessary. An amphitheatre was primarily meant for entertainment and would have been the venue for gladiatorial contests as well as games and military training. There may also have been wild animal fights, though probably not with exotic animals such as lions and tigers. More likely, for a fortress and town on the edge of the Empire, the Romans would have used animals then found in the local area: wolves, bears, wild boars and cattle.

At the fortress of Isca remains include parts of the walls with turrets incorporated into them, and the foundations of barrack blocks, thought to be the only legionary barrack blocks now visible in Europe.

Caerleon Roman Amphitheatre

Dr R E M Wheeler (later Sir Mortimer Wheeler) and his wife Tessa carried out the excavation of the amphitheatre in 1926 and 1927.

The amphitheatre was built of stone and would have had a wooden superstructure to take the seating. The arena was oval and was about 56 metres long by 41 metres broad. There were eight entrances into the arena, two main processional entrances at either end, and six smaller entrances with direct access to the seating area. This would enable soldiers watching events in the amphitheatre to have easy access to the arena to participate in any activities. Of particular interest is a small room blocking the eastern side-entrance. This has stone seats and a brick niche where a statue or altar could have been placed. It has been identified as a waiting room where gladiators or other contestants remained until it was their turn to enter the arena.

On early maps of Caerleon the amphitheatre field is known as the Round Table Field, and there are strong literary connections between Caerleon and the legends of King Arthur. It is certainly a logical possibility that it was a meeting place for a post-Roman military ruler and his army and, unlike a famous wooden Round Table at Winchester, the amphitheatre would have been in existence in Arthur's time.

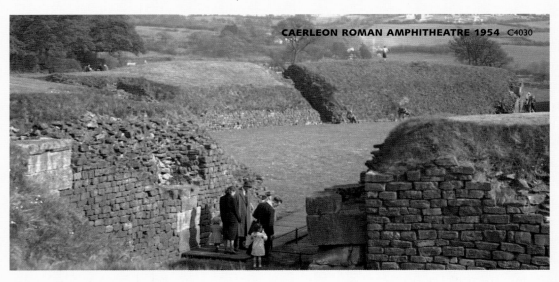

CAERLEON ROMAN AMPHITHEATRE 1954   C4030

Originally there would have been 60 blocks like this to provide sleeping accommodation for all the soldiers of the Legion.

The pride of Roman Isca must have been the fortress baths. These were built on a very grand scale near the centre at about the time it was founded in AD75. They are, in fact, a complex of facilities consisting of a massive hall containing plunge baths at different temperatures, a courtyard with an outdoor swimming pool and adjacent to a huge basilica or exercise hall. It is clear that it was not only the soldiers who used the baths, as a drain underneath contained women's jewellery, gem stones from finger rings and even infants' milk teeth. In 1188 Gerald of Wales, a cleric travelling through Caerleon, remarked of the fortress:

'There are immense palaces, which, with the gilded gables of their roofs, once rivalled the magnificence of ancient Rome. ... There is a lofty tower, and besides it remarkable hot baths, the remains of temples and an amphitheatre. All this is enclosed within impressive walls, parts of which still remain standing. Wherever you look, both within and without the circuit of these walls, you can see constructions dug deep into the earth, conduits for water, underground passages and air-vents'.

The fortress baths survived as a ruined shell until the 12th or 13th century when they were demolished during the rebuilding of Caerleon Castle. Today the excavated remains of the swimming pool and part of the huge bathhouse, where the cold plunge baths were situated, are on display in a modern exhibition building. However it is not surprising that visitors to the ruined fortress should have associated it with the stories of King Arthur. Geoffrey of Monmouth in his 'History of the Kings of Britain' claimed that Arthur held court at Caerleon, and that the town was the site of an ancient archbishopric. It was here also that two early Christian martyrs, Aaron and Julius, are said to have been killed during the Roman persecution of the 3rd century. Later chapels were set up dedicated to these saints. Today the name of Julius is still commemorated in the name of the Newport suburb of St Julians.

Did you know?
Roman Barrack Blocks
There are four Roman barrack blocks still to be seen in Caerleon, but only one of them is on the original ground level. The excavators had so much spoil that they covered over the site of three of the barrack blocks and relaid the stone foundations on top.

Did you know?
Caerleon Excavations
The excavation of Caerleon amphitheatre involved the removal of so much overlaying soil that a railway line had to be constructed. The excavators pushed trucks along the railway line through one of the main entrances to the amphitheatre and dumped their spoil to south of the site, building up low-lying land near to the river.

Newport appears to have developed as a settlement in the 6th century. The earliest settlement would have been on top of Stow Hill. Following the collapse of Roman rule a number of small kingdoms were established in South Wales. According to tradition, the local area west of the Usk was ruled in the 6th century by a king called Gwynllyw, giving his name to the kingdom of Gwynllŵg (later known as Wentlooge).

There are many different legends associated with Gwynllyw. In one version he seized Gwladys, the daughter of the King of Brecon, and took her as his wife. He also had a reputation as a robber and a thief.

Site of the early Welsh Church founded by Gwynllyw.

ST WOOLOS CHURCH 1899 43663

One night he sent some of his men to Caerwent to seize a cow belonging to St Tathan, an Irish hermit living there. The next day Tathan came to demand his cow back and so impressed Gwynllyw that they became close friends, and Gwynllyw gave his son Cadoc to Tathan to be educated. Cadoc grew up to become a famous holy man and founded a monastery at Llancarfan in Glamorgan.

In another story Gwynllyw was persuaded to repent of his ways by Tathan and decided to build a church on Stow Hill. One day he found a white ox with a black spot on its forehead. He took the ox as an omen that this was the site where he should build the church. The church is now the cathedral church of St Woolos (Woolos being a corruption of the name Gwynllyw). Gwynllyw and Gwladys lived nearby, possibly re-occupying the Iron Age hill fort of the Gaer, and when Gwynllyw died, Cadoc buried him in his own church. Modern Newport therefore began on Stow Hill.

Did you know?
Animal Bones
When the Roman fortress baths were excavated between 1971 and 1988, large quantities of small animal bones were found. They were identified as those of shrews, voles, mice and small birds regurgitated by barn owls that had been using the building as a roost after its abandonment by the Roman army.

CAERLEON ROMAN AMPHITHEATRE 1954 C4030

CHAPTER TWO

Of Kings and Princes

THE SMALL kingdoms established after the end of Roman rule often owed allegiances to larger kingdoms, and South Wales was no exception. The Welsh kingdoms were frequently under threat, both from internal fighting and external invasion. The kingdom of Gwent (east of the Usk) was ruled in the early 7th century by a king called Tewdrig. Sometime about 625 Tewdrig defeated a Saxon army, probably near to modern Tintern, securing much of south Wales from Saxon conquest and allowing Stow Hill to survive for many years as a Welsh settlement.

Saxon incursions were not the only threat to early Newport. A written account of the time, the 'Anglo-Saxon Chronicle', also records Viking raids into south Wales such as the major raid in 914-915:

'In this year a great pirate host came over hither from the south from Brittany under two earls, Ohtor and Harold, and sailed west about until they reached the estuary of the Severn … They were opposed by men from Hereford and Gloucester who put them to flight. … They encamped out on the island of Steepholm until the time came that they were very short of food, and many men perished of hunger'.

Indeed, the burial of a Viking warrior was found at nearby Caerwent. There can be no doubt that the people of the Newport area would have been threatened by these raiders and other raids. In 1049 another major raid up the River Usk is recorded:

'In this year thirty six [Viking] ships came from Ireland up the Welsh Usk, and did evil thereabout, aided by Gruffydd, the Welsh king. Forces were gathered against them, and bishop Ealdred went with them, but they had too few troops, and the enemy took them by surprise when it was quite early in the morning and slew many good men there, and the others made their escape with the bishop'.

In 1878, during the construction of a new timber pond for the Newport Alexandra Dock, workmen discovered the remains of a timber vessel about twelve feet below the surface. Local antiquarian, Octavius Morgan, identified it as an ancient Viking boat, probably associated with the 10th century Viking raids. Radiocarbon dating in 1979 appeared to confirm his identification and suggested a date around 950. However later examination of the tree rings showed that this date came from old wood near the centre of a tree trunk and that the boat may have been built after the Norman conquest. Nevertheless, it was a remarkable early find.

Did you know?
Viking Boat Construction

A Viking boat was built by making a hull of overlapping planks by a method known as clinker built. Then frames (ribs) were inserted inside the hull. This tradition of boat building continued into the 15th century, which is the date of a large medieval ship also found at Newport. By the 16th century most ships were built with the frames forming a skeleton first and the outer hull added without the planks overlapping. This was known as carvel built.

A NORMAN SHIP ZZZ01294

At the time of the Norman Conquest, Gwynllŵg (the area of Newport west of the Usk) was a cantref or division of the kingdom of Morgannwg. This kingdom stretched to the west from the River Usk and across modern Glamorgan, but the cantrefs or cantrefi were, to a great extent, independent units.

The first Norman to be involved in the conquest of south Wales was William fitz Osbern, who had been created Earl of Hereford by William the Conqueror. Fitz Osbern invaded the kingdom of Gwent (the land east of the Usk) and captured territory including land once belonging to Harold Godwin, the former Earl of Hereford and King of England, who died at the battle of Hastings in 1066.

In 1081 William the Conqueror marched across south Wales, often with the acceptance of local Welsh rulers, but it was left to Robert fitz Hamon to begin the conquest of the kingdom of Morgannwg in 1093. Though much of south Wales still remained in Welsh hands, there were feuds and fighting involving both Normans and Welsh for many years to come.

Did you know?
Stow Hill

Newport's first castle on Stow Hill suffered from attacks on several occasions by the Welsh. In 1172 Iorwerth ap Owain, Lord of Caerleon, attacked Newport after the murder of his son. Again in 1183 there was a major Welsh attack on castles at Neath, Kenfig, Newcastle (South Wales), Bridgend, Cardiff and Rumney. The castle also changed hands because of disputes between Norman barons and the king and in 1265 Simon de Montfort seized the castle during a barons' revolt.

INTERIOR OF ST WOOLOS CHURCH 1932 N25120
This church is now a cathedral. The west doorway and nave date to the 12th century.

William Rufus, the son of William the Conqueror, created Fitz Hamon Earl of Gloucester, and Robert of Hay controlled Newport for him. It was probably Robert of Hay who was responsible for the first castle at Newport, on an earth mound built on top of Stow Hill, not far from St Woolos Church. This mound was totally buried in the 1840s by spoil from the building of the nearby railway tunnel.

Newport, including Wentlooge, was a marcher lordship. This meant that the lord had many powers similar to the previous Welsh rulers. A marcher lord could build castles, raise armies and might have much greater control over the area than the king himself.

Robert fitz Hamon died in 1107. His son, also called Robert, succeeded him and he in turn he was succeeded by his son William. As William died without an heir, the lordship changed hands and was eventually acquired by Richard of Clare, third Earl of Hereford. The Clares were immensely powerful and when Earl Gilbert de Clare died at the Battle of Bannockburn in 1314 the Clare estates were divided up. Gilbert had three daughters, Eleanor who married Hugh Despenser the Younger, Margaret who married Hugh Audley, and Elizabeth who married Roger Damory. These sons-in-law had violent disputes over control of the Clare lands. In 1320 Hugh Audley had given up a claim to Newport to Hugh Despenser in exchange for other lands in England. However, in May 1321 Hugh Audley, Roger Damory and other lords attacked Newport Castle and Despenser castles in south Wales. Many, including Newport, were seized. State papers of the time record:

'800 men at arms, with the King's banner of arms displayed, and with 500 hobelers and 10,000 footmen … besieged the towns and castles, and took them by force, and slew part of his men … of the said Hugh le Spenser … they imprisoned and held to ransom those who refused, and burnt their houses and goods. And during the same time they wasted all his manors and robbed him of all his moveables therein'. (A hobeler was a light horseman.)

Hugh Despenser and his father, Hugh Despenser the Elder, were favourites of the king, Edward II, but the Despensers' greed

A MEDIEVAL KNIGHT AND HIS LADY, FROM A TOMB IN INGHAM CHURCH, NORFOLK ZZZ01295

caused resentment by other lords so that they were forced into exile in the summer of 1321. However, Edward II's opponents' success was short-lived for, on 22 March 1322, they were defeated at the battle of Boroughbridge. The leader of the opposition, the Earl of Lancaster, was beheaded, Roger Damory was also executed and Hugh Audley was imprisoned. Hugh Despenser the Younger reacquired his lands in south Wales, including Newport.

In 1324 the town of Newport, together with other towns controlled by Hugh Despenser, received a charter granting various freedoms from tolls.

In 1327 King Edward II was deposed and murdered. Despenser was tried and executed and Hugh Audley regained Newport and other possessions. Audley was a loyal servant of the

ARTIST'S IMPRESSION OF JOUSTING KNIGHTS ZZZ01296

new king, Edward III, acting for a time as the king's envoy in France and also fighting for him in Ireland. There may have been a new castle built at Newport, by the river to protect the bridge and the developing town next to it.

Newport Castle

The Welsh name for Newport is Casnewydd, meaning new castle. In the Middle Ages Newport was also called by its Latin name of Novus Burgus, meaning new burgh or new town. This implies the moving of the town from the top of Stow Hill to the edge of the Usk, close to the new castle and the bridge.

NEWPORT CASTLE IN 1793 ZZZ01401
(Courtesy of www.newportpast.com)
This shows the wooden town bridge.

THE BRIDGE 1893 32630
Newport Castle as it looked in 1893.

Audley had one daughter, Margaret. As the heiress to considerable property she attracted the attention of Hugh Stafford, one of Audley's companions. Stafford abducted Margaret and married her. Despite initial outrage on the part of his new father-in-law, Stafford eventually became Earl of Gloucester, raised to the title by Henry IV.

Hugh Audley died in 1347 so possession of Newport and other territories passed to Hugh Stafford, who was created first Earl of Stafford. The Staffords retained Newport for most of the next 200 years. In April 1385, Hugh Stafford, second Earl of Stafford, granted Newport a charter confirming that the town had many privileges, including the right to hold courts and to control aspects of trade. The burgesses could also hold a weekly market and an annual fair beginning on 9 August. A guild controlled the borough regulations and the chief official was called a Reeve (the title was later changed to Mayor).

The Earl also founded a Friary in Newport in 1377, near the present bus station, and this is still commemorated in the road names Austin Friars and Friars Street. Two other chapels or chantries also existed in the town.

The Earls of Stafford continued the tradition of active service for the crown, and Edmund Stafford, fifth Earl of Stafford, became involved in the campaigns against the rebellion of Owain Glyndŵr. In 1403 Newport was attacked and the town destroyed by the rebels. Edmund himself had been killed during the battle of Shrewsbury on 21 July 1403, leaving a one year-old son as his heir.

Humphrey Stafford, the sixth Earl of Stafford, inherited a town devastated by the rebels. His revenues from Newport went down to nothing and it took many years for Newport to regain its prosperity. In 1421 he was old enough to take control of his lands and in 1427 granted a charter confirming Newport's privileges. Newport castle had been neglected and an active programme of rebuilding was begun. The Newport Castle of today, with its three towers overlooking the river, dates from this period.

Humphrey Stafford was a great supporter of the king, Henry VI, and was created Duke of Buckingham in 1444. He fought for the king in France and against the Yorkists during the Wars of the Roses. When he was killed in the Battle of Northampton in 1460 his lands passed to his grandson, Henry. Henry was still a small boy, so his lands were taken into royal custody. Such lands would often be farmed out to other landowners until the heir became of age.

The new Yorkist king, Edward IV, had dethroned Henry VI. In 1461 he granted custody of Newport to William Herbert of Raglan Castle, who made Newport very profitable by imprisoning people who owed him money in Newport Castle. Richard Neville, Earl of Warwick executed Herbert in 1469. Neville, known as Warwick the Kingmaker, had aided Edward IV in his seizure of the throne, but was eventually to turn against him. Forced to flee Britain in March 1470, he returned in October to depose Edward IV and re-instate Henry VI as King. He was, in turn, defeated and killed at the Battle of Barnet in April 1471. Edward IV regained the kingdom and Henry VI was killed.

Medieval Ship

MEDIEVAL SHIP ZZZ01396 (Bob Trett)

Excavation of the Newport Medieval Ship in August 2002.

RECONSTRUCTION OF THE NEWPORT SHIP ZZZ01397

How the ship might have looked, drawn by Anne Leaver from an original drawing by Owain Roberts.

A chance discovery in 2002 relates to this interesting period. During the building of a new Arts Centre for Newport, on the edge of the Usk, the remains of a large medieval ship were found. After an intense campaign in the city, money was found to excavate the ship and remove the timbers for eventual re-display in Newport.

What the ship was doing in Newport is a mystery. It appears to have been a large ocean going vessel, and the finds inside the ship included Portuguese pottery and coins. By dating wood found under the ship it was possible to work out that it was brought to Newport in 1469 or soon after. This coincides with the time when Warwick the Kingmaker had control over the kingdom and was also in charge of Newport. Warwick also had a private fleet that at times was very active in piracy, even seizing on occasion Portuguese ships. Could this be a ship captured by Warwick's fleet? One clue was discovered in a letter signed by the Earl of Warwick dated 22 November 1469. In the letter Warwick authorises payments:

'£10 unto John Colt for the making of the ship at Newport, to Richard Port purser of the same 53 shillings 4 pence, to William Toker mariner for the carriage of iron (nails) from Cardiff unto Newport for the said ship 6 shillings and 8 pence, to Matthew Jubber in money, iron, salt and other stuff belonging to the said ship £15 two shillings and six pence'.

These were sums that might be needed for

repairs to a large ship and Matthew Jubber might be selling the contents. What we do know is that the Newport Ship had extensive damage. There had been attempts to repair it before it was abandoned and partly dismantled. Whatever the truth, Newport has the most complete 15th century ship to survive in Europe and a major future attraction to the city.

Henry, second Duke of Buckingham, granted Newport another charter in 1473, although there is no evidence that he ever visited the town. He is best known for his support of Richard III, who seized the throne in 1483. Henry may have had no involvement in the murder of the Princes in the Tower, and he attempted to stage a rebellion against Richard soon after his succession. The rebellion was a failure and Henry was executed.

After Richard III's death at the Battle of Bosworth in 1485, Margaret the widow of Henry, second Duke of Buckingham, married Jasper Tudor, uncle to the new king Henry VII. Her own son Edward was still a child and it may be Jasper Tudor that carried out much of the rebuilding of St Woolos Church. A statue in the wall of the church tower is thought to be of him. Edward, third Duke of Buckingham, came of age in 1483 but he was the third duke to die a violent death. In 1521 he was executed for treason and his lands and estates, including Newport, confiscated by the King. The Lordship of Newport remained in royal control until the Act of Union in 1536, when the old lordships were abolished.

At the time of the third Duke's death in 1521 a survey of his lands was carried out. From this we have a description of Newport:

'The toune of Newport is a burg and a p(ro)pur toune and haith a goodly haven commyng unto hit, well occupied with small Crayes whereunto a veray great shippe may resoorte and have good harbour.

A STATUE ON THE TOWER OF ST WOOLOS CHURCH 1893
32632x

Thought to be Jasper Tudor.

You can still see the coat of arms of the former Borough of Newport around the city. Newport Transport buses use it as their crest and it features on plaques on the Town Bridge and elsewhere. The crest shows a shield with a red chevron upside down on a gold background. Above this is the face a winged cherub. The shield is derived from those of the Stafford Dukes of Buckingham, but the chevron is reversed since the third duke was executed for treason. The full coat of arms has supporters of a winged lion and a dragon, both with fish tails, illustrating Newport's links with the sea and with both England and Wales. The motto Terra Marique means 'by land and sea'. In fact, Newport did not receive its full coat of arms until 1958.

CREST OF THE FORMER BOROUGH OF NEWPORT ZZZ01393

Upon the same haven is a proper Castell and III towers adjoining juste to the water. The middelleste tower having a vowte or entre to receive into the Castell a good vessell.'

A cray was a small trading ship. In 1994 part of a small trading vessel was discovered in the Severn Estuary at Magor Pill, not far from Newport. This was recovered by the National Museum of Wales and the timbers dated to about 1240. Like the Newport Ship it could well have used one of the creeks or pills of Newport as a harbour. The main harbour would have been the Town Pill, a little to the south of Newport Bridge. Now all that remains of this inlet that once stretched into the centre of the town is an indent in the river wall by the modern Steel Wave sculpture.

Even today we can recognise the description of the castle, with its three towers and the arched vault (vowte) with access to the river, allowing ships to unload.

THE GREAT TOWER AND WATER GATE OF NEWPORT CASTLE 1932 N25110

Before restoration.

YE OLDE MURENGER HOUSE c1950 N25139

The wooden town bridge stood alongside the castle, and one of three gates that guarded access to the town. Another of the gates was on the site of the Westgate Hotel (now a shopping complex). A third gate stood to the north of the town. Whether Newport had a proper stone wall is not known, although foundations of what could be the walls are still visible in the cellars of Yates Wine Bar (formerly the Tredegar Arms) in High Street.

In High Street stands one of Newport's oldest houses, Ye Olde Murenger House. This timber-framed house is believed to date to the 16th century and was originally the town house of Sir Charles Herbert, the first Sheriff of the new county of Monmouthshire. The Murenger House is now an inn. A murenger was an official responsible for the upkeep of the town walls, but there is no evidence of one being in existence at the time the house was built. Maybe the name was invented when the house changed use in the 19th century.

Newport was primarily a crossing point over the Usk, a small market town and a port. In the Middle Ages most of its trade was with Bristol, the main customs port for the Severn and also from places further up the River Usk. Exports would have included cloth, skins and foodstuffs, and wine, salt and iron would have been among the many items imported. Newport ships are recorded as bringing salted fish from Ireland and brass and pewter-ware from Bristol - and of course, in common with many Welsh ports, Newport ships would have smuggled goods to avoid paying royal taxes.

A TUDOR SHIP FROM THE TIME OF HENRY VIII, AFTER HOLBEIN ZZZ01290

By the 16th century Newport was becoming more important as a port. In Elizabeth I's reign there are records of two ships of over 100 tons as well as many small ships. No other port in the Severn apart from Bristol had any ships of over 100 tons. And it was during Elizabeth's reign that David Roberts, controller of customs for Newport, was accused of receiving pirates and their spoils! The town's connection with the sea continues to the present day, as we will see.

Another relic of Newport's medieval past was discovered in 1925 when a finely decorated stone cross head was found buried in the mud of the River Usk, near to Newport Bridge. Originally it would have been lantern-shaped, but it had been deliberately sliced in half. The surviving piece depicts a Crucifixion scene, and the side panels show St Catherine and St Margaret spearing a dragon.

The cross head dates to the 15th century and was thought to come from a wayside cross. These were put up along roadsides sometimes to mark boundaries, but often for the use of pilgrims on their way to visit holy shrines. One is known to have existed on Stow Hill and it was thought that this may be where the cross head originally came from. However the cross head is very grand and may have come from a more important setting such as a churchyard or a market place.

In April 2004 a new town cross was erected in Newport High Street, near where an original market cross could have stood. The new cross includes an exact reproduction of the surviving piece, carefully completed to look as it might have done in the 15th century. The original crosshead is on display in Newport Museum.

Why was the cross head pulled down and damaged? It could have happened during the Reformation, in about 1537, when the crown seized buildings and land belonging to the Austin Friars in Newport. Alternatively it could be part of the damage done by Puritans during the Civil War against Charles I. Perhaps only a strong belief that such an item was idolatrous could have made anyone go to such lengths to destroy this fine cross.

Did you know?
Newport's Ships
During Queen Elizabeth I's reign Newport had nine ships of over 20 tons. These were the Green Dragon and the White Eagle, both 100 tons, the Griffan and the Lyon, both 40 tons, the Black Lyon, 34 tons, the Steven and the Samuell, both 30 tons, and the Mary Rose 26 tons. (This Mary Rose is not the famous Tudor warship of the same name.)

COPY OF 15TH CENTURY CROSS 2004
N25702k (Bob Trett)

This copy of a 15th century cross was unveiled in Newport High Street in 2004.

THE GREAT TOWER AND WATER GATE OF NEWPORT CASTLE 1932 N25110

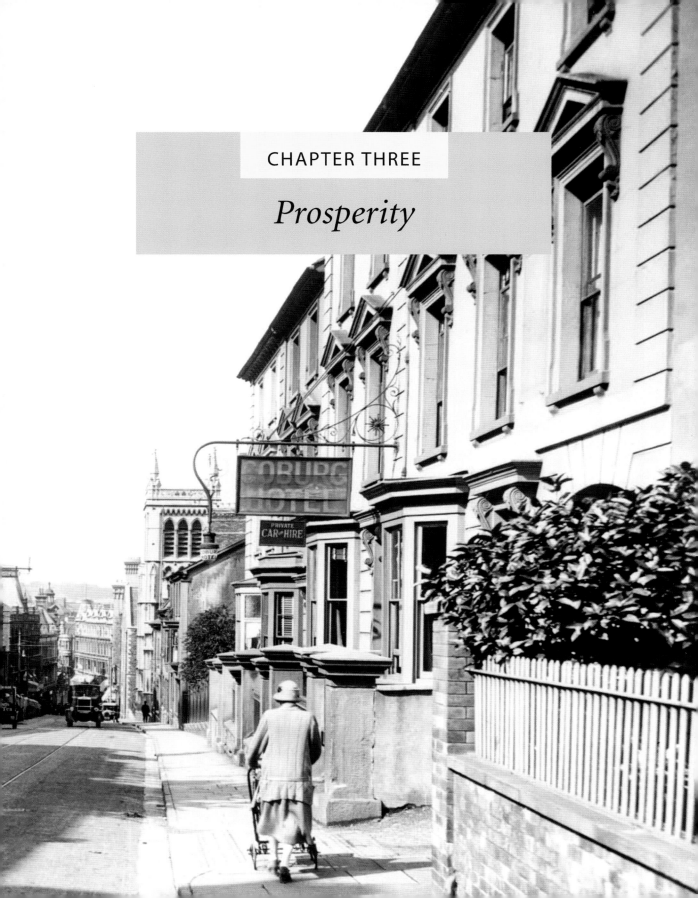

CHAPTER THREE

Prosperity

DURING THE 15th century the Morgan family of Tredegar House were rising to the prominent position they were to have in the affairs of Newport. As the family had many branches there were Morgans living in several of the castles and large houses in south Wales.

The family fortunes fluctuated. The Morgans supported the Lancastrian King Henry IV in his struggle to gain the throne and were able to acquire more lands, including some in the western valleys of South Wales.

At the time these lands may have been of no great value but centuries later they were to be the source of great wealth from mining. In 1402 Llywelyn ap Morgan had supported Owain Glyndŵr in his rebellion against Henry IV. As a result he lost all his lands to the crown but by making a good political marriage for his son he managed to get them restored.

In 1485 Sir John Ap Morgan supported Henry Tudor in his successful bid for the crown. He was well rewarded and able to increase his wealth and influence. About this time a stone hall was built on the site just west of Newport. King Charles I visited this hall in 1645, after his defeat at the Battle of Naseby. Part of this building still exists and is now the servants' hall attached to Tredegar House.

Tredegar House and the Morgans

Thomas Morgan of Plas Machen inherited Tredegar in 1653. It is he who probably started to rebuild Tredegar House, but as he died in 1666, it is likely that his son, Sir William Morgan built most of the new house. The work was completed in 1672 and the new Tredegar House was, and still is, a very grand house with state rooms, fine bedrooms, a large park and all the requirements needed by a rich family of landed gentry. The Morgans continued to accumulate land to enjoy their lifestyle and inherited wealth from relatives such as John Morgan of Ruperra Castle, who had become rich from the shipping trade. Jane Morgan, who was married to Sir Charles Gould, a successful lawyer and judge, inherited the estate in 1792. On gaining the Tredegar inheritance Sir Charles was granted the name and arms of Morgan and given a baronetcy. He then began developing the commercial and industrial potential of the Tredegar Estates. He took advantage of coalmining and iron working in South Wales, and he invested in the construction of the Monmouthshire Canal and the Brecknock and Abergavenny Canal. He also owned land where the Sirhowy to Newport Tramroad crossed through his park. The tramway had been authorised by an Act of Parliament in 1802 and completed a few years later and became known as the Golden Mile because of the profits he made from the tolls on horse pulled trucks crossing his land. He charged 'one halfpenny for every ton of coal or stone, one penny a ton for iron and two pence a ton for general merchandise'.

The buccaneer Sir Henry Morgan is believed to have been one relative of the Morgans of Tredegar House. As a young man he went to sea and rose to the rank of Admiral. When he became Lieutenant Governor of Jamaica he was famous (or notorious) for attacks on the Spanish in the Caribbean, including the sacking of Puerto Bello near Panama. He died in Jamaica in 1684, but there is no evidence that he ever visited his kinsmen at Tredegar House.

TREDEGAR HOUSE, THE NORTHWEST FRONT FROM THE STABLE BLOCK 2004
N25703k (Bob Trett)

Did you know?

John Wesley

In 1739 John Wesley visited Newport and stopped in Westgate Square to preach. He noted in his diary that he found the citizens of Newport the 'most insensible, ill-behaved' people he had ever seen. However he must have been effective since on a return visit in 1775 he wrote: 'I believe it is five and thirty years since I preached here before to a people who were then as wild as boars. How amazingly the scene has changed'.

The canals were the stimulus for Newport's development from a small trading town with a population of about 1,087 in 1801, to a large industrial and commercial centre with a population of 67,270 in 1901.

In 1792 an Act of Parliament authorised the construction of the Monmouthshire Canal. This consisted of a main line 11 miles long from Newport to Pontnewynydd via Pontypool, and a branch to Crumlin, which left the main line at Malpas just outside Newport. The canal (serviced by a network of tramroads for horse-pulled trucks) was officially opened in 1799, although parts of the canal were already open. It allowed coal and iron to be transported to Newport much more efficiently, but it was also used for other goods including timber, lime and farm produce.

THE CANAL AT ALT-YR-YN 1893 32637

Did *you* know?
Canal Traffic

In 1798 almost 44,000 tons of goods were carried by canal. In the first quarter of the 19th century, the age of the canal, up to 1,100 barges used it. Each barge could carry between 25 and 28 tons. The Blaenavon Ironworks alone sent 300 tons of iron a week by canal.

Whilst the town's prosperity increased, there were also changes in its government. The Act of Union of 1536 had stripped the old lordship of its political power and Newport was joined to other former lordships to create the County of Monmouthshire. A Sheriff was appointed and the Mayor of Newport, assisted by Justices of the Peace, had considerable legal authority. In 1623 King James I granted a new charter to Newport. This set up a Corporation in Newport, which consisted of townsmen to maintain good government in the town. A Mayor and twelve Aldermen held the authority, and the first Mayor was John Priddy. The Mayor held office for one year and Aldermen held office for life. A Recorder was also appointed to give legal advice to the Corporation.

This system eventually changed in 1835, when the Municipal Corporations Act was passed. Under this, all boroughs were governed by a uniform system, with a Mayor, Aldermen and a Town Council elected by rate paying citizens. It was the beginning of modern local government.

One of the most memorable events in Newport's history happened on Sunday 3 November 1839 when about 5,000 men marched down Stow Hill and massed outside the Westgate Hotel. John Frost, a former Mayor

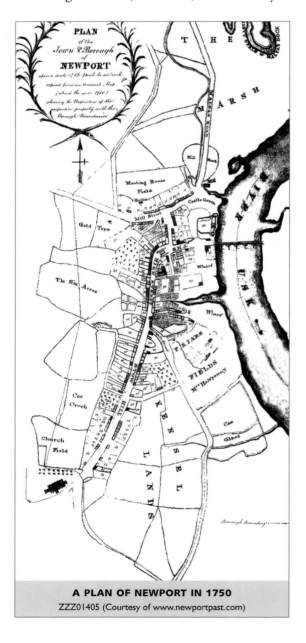

A PLAN OF NEWPORT IN 1750
ZZZ01405 (Courtesy of www.newportpast.com)

another issue, there was no possibility of the Chartists' demands being considered at that time. This led to anger and frustration and there were alarming threats of armed insurrection. On the 12 July the House of Commons refused by 235 to 46 votes to consider the national petition.

This was the time of the industrial revolution and economic recession. There were appalling working conditions in many of the South Wales coalmines and ironworks. Workers were hired and fired at the will of the owners. Men, women and children, some only five years old, could be working up to fourteen hours a day. A national strike failed to materialise but discontent in South Wales led to the last armed uprising on mainland Britain.

There was a history of violence and unrest in the South Wales Valleys and John Frost believed that an outbreak in Wales would be supported by insurrections in Yorkshire and Lancashire. This failed to happen. Nevertheless, on the night of 3 - 4 November several thousand Welsh Chartists gathered for a march on Newport. Outside the Westgate Hotel they shouted for the release of some Newport men imprisoned within its cellars. What they did not know was that about 30 soldiers of the 45th Regiment were defending the Hotel. A shot was fired and a scuffle followed. The soldiers then fired volleys at Chartists attempting to break into the Hotel and also at those who were outside. The marchers broke up and fled, but it is thought that 22 of them were left dead and were later buried outside St Woolos Church.

of Newport, led men from Blackwood, Zephaniah Williams came with men from Ebbw Vale and William Jones with men from Pontypool. They had come to demand political changes included in the People's Charter.

The People's Charter was a national campaign set up to improve Parliamentary representation for the working classes. The Chartists had six demands:

· **Annual parliaments**
· **Universal male suffrage**
· **Equal electoral districts**
· **Removal of property qualifications for members of parliament**
· **Secret ballots**
· **Payment of members of parliament**

A national petition was presented to Parliament on 6 May 1839 but, as the Government resigned on the 7 May on

THE CANAL AT ALT-YR-YN 1893 32637

STOW HILL 1932 N25114

This was the route taken by the Chartist marches in 1839.

The leaders of the Chartists, including John Frost, Zephaniah Williams and William Jones were soon arrested, but more soldiers were brought to the area to protect the local landowners who were still nervous. With the extra protection the leading citizens of Newport celebrated with dinners and presentations. The Mayor, Thomas Phillips, was knighted and given a silver plaque with the names of grateful citizens inscribed on it. It was claimed at the time that:

'With the help of God, the mayor, and the small company of the 45th Regiment they had done their duty and saved not only South Wales but also Britain and the civilised world'.

Many of the Chartists were tried at the Westgate Hotel. Of the 125 prisoners appearing on charges, well over half were discharged and a dozen given short gaol sentences, but the ring leaders, including John Frost, were charged with high treason and sent to the county gaol at Monmouth. The three Chartist leaders were convicted and sentenced to be hanged and quartered. However, their sentences were later changed to transportation to a convict settlement in

Tasmania for life and in 1854 they received a pardon. John Frost returned to Britain in 1856, but Zephaniah Williams and William Jones remained in Australia.

Although the Chartists appeared to have failed, conditions did begin to improve. There was an economic boom in the South Wales coalfields in the 1850s and 1860s, giving greater prosperity. In addition, new regulations and better awareness brought about improved working conditions. As for the political demands of the Charter, all (with the exception of annual parliaments) are now the law of the land. John Frost is today Newport's most celebrated hero and the main square in the City is named after him. Few remember Thomas Phillips.

HIGH STREET c1950 25184

The Westgate Hotel is on the left.

HIGH STREET c1950 25184

Early Canal Boat

In 1984 Mr John Evans, a farmer at Tredunnoc some miles north of Newport and Caerleon, noticed a large boat protruding from beneath a bank of the River Usk. The boat was excavated by the Glamorgan Gwent Archaeological Trust in 1987. The archaeologists were hoping to lift it out of the river and take it to Newport for conservation and eventual display. Just days before a crane was due to undertake the delicate business of lifting the boat, a flash flood in the Usk dragged the boat off the river bed, carrying it 100 yards downriver before it was smashed to pieces on the riverbank.

Luckily it was possible to salvage much of the vessel, which proved to be a very early canal boat, some 18 metres long, double-ended and flat bottomed. It would have had a small mast for towing along from a canal or riverbank and its structure suggested that it had been constructed early in the 19th century. The only access from the canal to the River Usk was at Newport Docks. Was this a canal boat no longer needed for its original purpose? Its condition suggested it had had a long life. The town dock, which gave the only access from the canal to the river, was not opened until 1842. By this time the railway had superseded the canal, but a river trade in timber still continued between Newport and Tredunnoc. The Tredunnoc boat could have been used for this trade before being abandoned and left to provide extra protection to the banks of the River Usk.

Canal boats of this date are exceedingly rare and it would be nice to think that one day the surviving sections of the boat may be put on public display, possibly at the Fourteen Locks Canal Centre.

PART OF THE LOCK SYSTEM AT FOURTEEN LOCKS 1896 38707 (Detail)

Fourteen Locks, on the Crumlin branch of the Monmouthshire Canal near Rogerstone, was part of a complex of locks, weirs and ponds to enable boats to rise or descend some 358 feet. In fact, the long step of locks was difficult to keep supplied with enough water to be effective, and competition from the new railway system hastened the decline of the canals.

With the advent of the railway, the canals began to fall into disrepair and parts were even closed, drained and used as the route for railways. Nevertheless, the Monmouthshire Canal lingered on and the last cargo was carried on the Crumlin arm in 1930, and on the Pontnewynydd in 1938. The Crumlin branch closed in 1949 and the eastern branch was abandoned in 1962. The Fourteen Locks Canal Heritage Centre opened in 1976. More recently many improvements have been made to the disused canal network with the hope of eventually re-opening much of the canal for pleasure craft, leisure activities and tourism.

Newport's first experience of railways came in 1829 when steam locomotives replaced teams of horses on the Sirhowy tramroad, making it possible for a single locomotive to do in one day what had formerly taken six horses two days to do. By the 1840s railways linking most of the cities were being built. There was a great desire in South Wales to join the new network and to find an improved means of transport over the stagecoaches running along the toll roads built all around the area.

An Act of Parliament permitted the setting of the South Wales Railway, going from Chepstow through Newport and on to Swansea. Work started on 4 August 1846. By November 1848 a 742-yard long tunnel under Stow Hill had been finished. Work had also started on a wooden bridge to cross the River Usk, but on the 31 May 1848 there was a massive fire while the central arch was being put in position. Workmen were putting in iron bolts when one bolt, which had been heated to a remarkable degree, suddenly ignited and caused the timber to burst into flame. Within a matter of hours the whole structure was destroyed. A new bridge was built but, as a precaution, the pipes of the local water works were laid across the bridge so that there was always a source of water to

WRECK OF THE IRON STEAMER SEVERN AT NEWPORT BRIDGE 1844 ZZZ01400 (Courtesy of www.newportpast.com)

fight any future fires. The bridge had its centre spanned by an immense iron arch made in Birmingham. The South Wales Railway was completed and was officially opened on 18 June 1850 with a celebratory return excursion to Swansea.

In 1863 the South Wales Railway was incorporated into the Great Western Railway. Other railway lines followed. The Pontypool, Caerleon and Newport Railway was opened in 1874 and in 1876 it also was absorbed by the Great Western Railway.

Newport's development in the 19th century depended on shipping. Coal, iron and other goods brought to Newport by the canal that ran along the present Kingsway could be unloaded easily onto wharves fronting onto the river. By the 1830s, though, and despite the forest of ship masts that could be seen along long stretches of the riverbank, there was a great need for a dock. The riverbank was inconveniently affected by the rise and fall of the river tide, which put restrictions on when goods could be loaded and unloaded and meant that the larger sea-going vessels would not come to Newport.

The first Newport dock in Pillgwenlly opened on the 10 October 1842. It had cost about £200,000 to construct and covered an area of four and a half acres. The opening was celebrated with bands playing and a gas illumination of the words 'Newport Docks' and the Prince of Wales' plume. Before long the new dock, too, proved inadequate for demand and an extension, to cover an area of eleven and a half acres, was opened on 1 March 1858. The whole complex was called the Town Dock. It had an entrance lock 220 feet long and the dock itself was 1,753 long and 300 feet wide, with an average depth of 26 and a half feet.

The demand for more docks increased as trade grew. An 1865 Act of Parliament authorised the establishment of the Alexandra (Newport) Dock Company to construct an entirely new dock covering 29 acres, closer to the mouth of the river. The Alexandra North Dock was completed in 1875. It had a trumpet-shaped entrance 300 feet wide that led into the entrance lock and a dock 2,500 feet long and 500 feet wide with an average depth of 30 feet. Thus the largest ships of the time could visit Newport Docks.

The docks had their own railway lines linked to the Great Western Railway. With the success of the North Dock an ambitious scheme followed for the construction of the Alexandra South Dock, which was completed in 1914. The South Lock was 1,000 feet long by 100 feet wide, making it the largest sea lock in the world at that time. The Company also owned a Dry (Graving) Dock connected to the North Dock and there were six other private docks in the Port of Newport.

It was the Morgans of Tredegar Park who created much of modern Newport. When Sir Charles Morgan succeeded his father, Sir Charles Gould Morgan, in 1806 he continued his father's development of financial and commercial projects in Newport. By establishing the Tredegar Wharf Company he created many of the wharves on the banks of the Usk and built the Pillgwenlly area of Newport on what was marshland belonging to the Tredegar Estate. It was here that the Town Dock was situated.

THE QUAY 1861 ZZZ01399 (Courtesy of www.newportpast.com)

TOWN REACH 1893 32623

Sir Charles' first love, though, was agriculture and farming, and it was he who established the Tredegar Cattle Show and paid for the Newport Cattle Market, which opened in 1844.

His son, yet another Sir Charles, succeeded him in 1846 and was eventually granted a peerage to become the first Baron Tredegar in 1859, for his support of Tory Prime Minister, Benjamin Disraeli. His second son, Godfrey Charles, succeeded him in 1875 and is most remembered for taking part in and surviving the Charge of the Light Brigade in 1854, during the Crimean War.

NEWPORT DOCKS AND FLOATING CRANE c1955 N25181

NEWPORT DOCKS AND FLOATING CRANE c1955 N25181

Did you know?
Sir Briggs

The horse ridden by Godfrey Morgan, later to be Lord Tredegar, at the Charge of the Light Brigade was called Sir Briggs. After faithfully serving his master and having survived the Crimea, Sir Briggs eventually died and was buried in the Cedar Garden at Tredegar House. A memorial in the middle of the garden commemorates him.

At the time Godfrey died in 1913 his income was reputed to have been £1,000 a day. In addition to his commercial and property interests in Newport and elsewhere, he owned over 1,000 farms, had mining rights in three counties and gave away £40,000 a year to worthy causes.

His gifts to Newport included the Tredegar and Belle Vue Parks, the playing fields at the Newport High School, the site of the Technical College, the ground for many of Newport's Churches and Chapels and the site of the Royal Gwent Hospital. He funded excavations at the Roman Town of Caerwent and gifted in his will the many discoveries to Newport Museum, which are now on display. He was also a supporter of the National Eisteddford that was hosted for the first time in Newport at Tredegar Park in 1897. He was a caring landlord and very popular with his tenants. One commented:

'In my boyhood I never heard anyone recall the old Viscount with anything but respect and real affection. After his death came the Great War and things were never the same again. His successors failed to occupy the same place in local hearts and minds'.

BELLE VUE PARK 1896 38700

VIEW OF NEWPORT 1896 38694

PART OF THE LOCK SYSTEM AT FOURTEEN LOCKS 1896 38707 (Detail)

BELLE VUE PARK 1896 38700

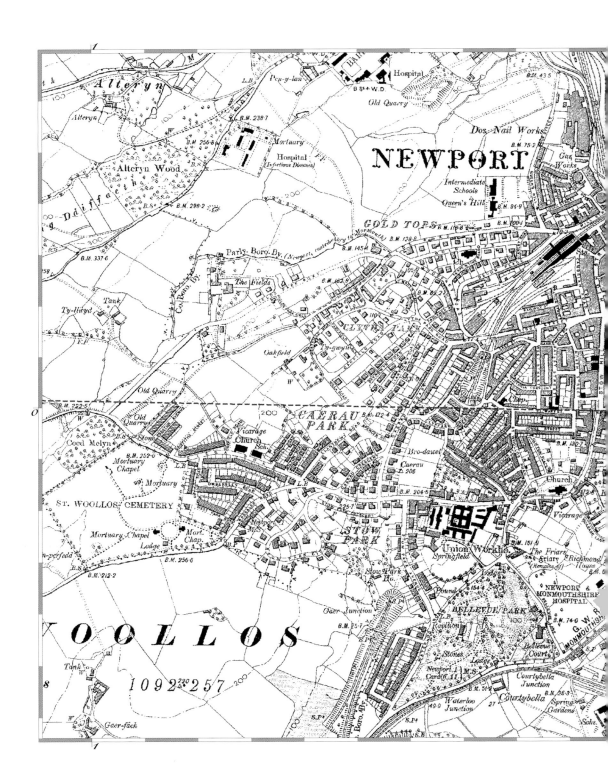

NEWPORT ORDNANCE SURVEY MAP 1900

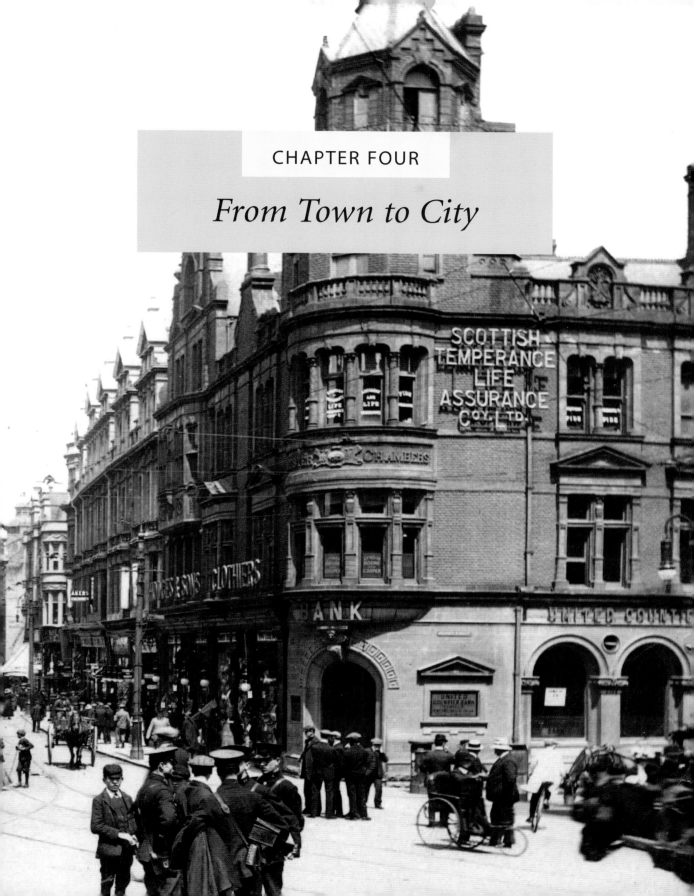

CHAPTER FOUR

From Town to City

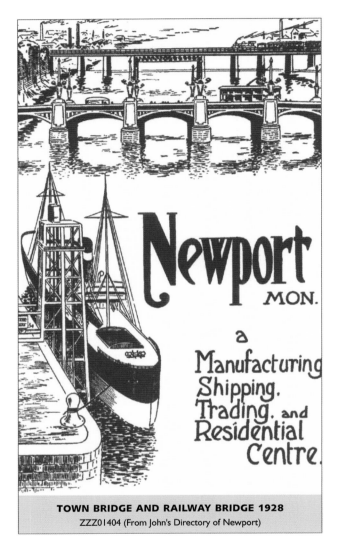

TOWN BRIDGE AND RAILWAY BRIDGE 1928
ZZZ01404 (From John's Directory of Newport)

uninhabited marshy area. With construction of the docks a new community was established. Pill, as it is known, was a new town with regular street patterns, uniform rows of houses and distinct commercial areas. This was very different from the higgledy-piggledy street pattern of the old town.

Among the most imposing features of the Victorian and Edwardian town were the numerous public and commercial buildings, many of which no longer survive. Newport's old Town Hall is one building that has now gone. It stood in Commercial Street on the site of what is now a concrete-fronted department store. When it was built in 1885 it cost about £35,000 and its principle feature was the 150-feet high clock tower, 150 feet high, a landmark that was visible from most of the town.

20TH-CENTURY NEWPORT would hardly have been recognisable to a visitor from 100 years earlier. In the 1800s the land east of the Usk would have been mainly open countryside. In 1900s the town sprawled both sides of the river. There were docks, factories, railways, roads, shops and houses, all reflecting the expansion of the town. Pilgwenlly, south of the town centre, had been a largely

HIGH STREET 1896   38696 (Detail)

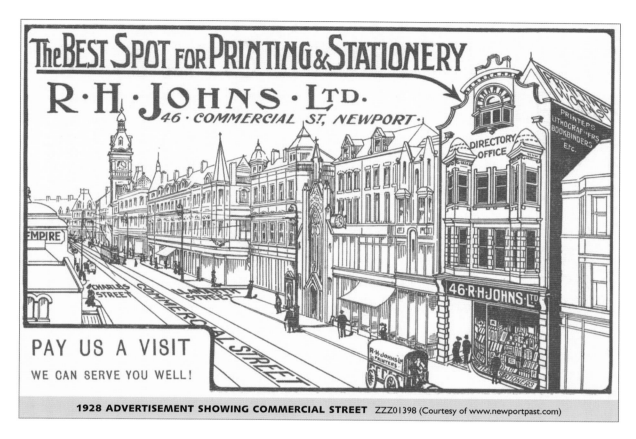

1928 ADVERTISEMENT SHOWING COMMERCIAL STREET   ZZZ01398 (Courtesy of www.newportpast.com)

COMMERCIAL STREET 1901   47896

Looking south. The Town Hall clock tower can be seen in the background.

SPECIALISED

TAILORING

ALEXANDRE

ALEXANDRE

COMMERCIAL STREET c1955 N25141

COMMERCIAL STREET, LOOKING NORTH 1910 62511

Wildings are still a leading Newport Store.

THE TOWN HALL CLOCK c1955 N25141 (Detail)

FREDK. J. ESCOTT,
Furniture Remover & General Haulier.

MAINDEE
FURNITURE
REPOSITORY

106 Chepstow
Rd., Newport.

FURNITURE
Bought, Sold, or
Exchanged.

Warehousing a Speciality

Furniture, Parcels, and Luggage collected and forwarded to and from all parts of the
Kingdom, by ROAD, RAIL or SEA.

ADVERTISEMENT FOR ESCOTT 1911 ZZZ1408
Courtesy of www.newportpast.com

Other buildings that have been lost include the Corn Exchange, erected in 1878 at the top of High Street and now the site of a multi storey car park, the old Library and Museum in Dock Street, most of the original Royal Gwent Hospital, opened in 1901 in Cardiff Road, and the columned Lyceum Theatre in Bridge Street.

SAVOY BUILDINGS 1910 62512

DETAIL OF OLD POST OFFICE BUILDING c1910

49481a (Detail)

The High Street with the Old Post Office and Corn Exchange.

ROYAL GWENT HOSPITAL 1901 47901 (Detail)

The main building.

Of the surviving Victorian and Edwardian buildings the most striking is the Provisions Market in Upper Dock Street. It was built between 1887 and 1889 and has a wide main hall and gallery, then able to house up to 150 stalls. The building, with its glass roof and its walls of red sandstone and its ornate tower, is still used for its original purpose and still retains its atmosphere. Other surviving buildings of the period include numerous churches and chapels such St Mark in Gold Tops (built in 1872-74), the Tredegar Estate Offices in Pentonville (built in 1905), the nearby Shire Hall (built in 1902 but extended in 1913), and the domed Technical Institute in Clarence Place (built 1909-10 but now empty).

THE VICTORIA ASSEMBLY ROOMS 1868
ZZZ01403 (Courtesy of www.newportpast.com)

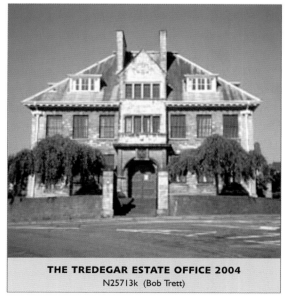

THE TREDEGAR ESTATE OFFICE 2004
N25713k (Bob Trett)

ST MARK'S CHURCH c1955 N25195

NEWPORT BRIDGE 1893 32630

The tower of the Provisions Market is in the background.

The buildings and others like them still reflect the prosperity of that era. Walking down High Street or Commercial Street the visitor has only to look above the ground floor shop fronts to see the decorated windows, balconies, columns, arches and spires in order to appreciate the splendour of Newport.

In 1900 the Corporation bought a former private residence and opened it as Beechwood Park. The town gradually gained many other leisure and educational facilities. Newport Rugby Football Club was formed in 1874 and games were played on the marshes until Lord Tredegar offered Newport Cricket, Athletic and Football Club land at a peppercorn rent. In 1841 the Newport Mechanics' Institute was opened for 'education and recreational efforts' and in 1851 a Newport Working Men's Institute was established. The first free library had been established in 1870, but a new building in Dock Street replaced it 1882 and in 1888 a Museum and Art Gallery was added to it. Thomas Phillips, John Frost's rival, was among the leading figures in the movement to provide schools and educational facilities for the rising population.

Belle Vue Park

Belle Vue Park on its 23 acres donated by Lord Tredegar in 1891 was laid out on the hillside overlooking the River Usk and the Severn Estuary. Designed by a leading Edwardian landscape architect, Thomas Mawson, after 'spirited' competition, it cost £19,500 to construct and was opened in September 1894. In 1896 a Gorsedd stone circle was added for the National Eisteddfod to be held in Newport in the following year.

The Newport Pictorial of 1906 reported: 'Besides finely undulating walks and convenient carriage drives, there are pavilion, conservatories, fountains, bandstand and terraces. There is also a well-fitted playground for children. A small ornamental lake with waterfall, admirably arranged, gives a pleasing variety; and sundry rock-work, rosary, and well-planned shrubberies, form with their accessories a coup d'oeil (view point) which would be difficult to surpass'.

Bottom Left:
WALKING IN BELLE VUE PARK 1932
N25118 (Detail)

Bottom Right:
THE BRIDGE IN BELLE VUE PARK 1896
38703 (Detail)

BELLE VUE PARK 1925 77456
View from the terrace

There were also other new services and transport systems during this period. Reservoirs were built at Ynys-y-Fro in 1847 and 1864 and in 1878 at Pant-yn-Eos. By 1888 Newport Corporation had acquired all three reservoirs and had to build a fourth at Wentwood that was completed in 1904. The four reservoirs contained 675,000,000 gallons of water when full.

There had been a gas supply as early as the 1820s that was gradually extended to provide lighting across most of Newport. The town's first electricity power station was opened in Llanarth Street in 1895. Seven years later the larger East Power Station was built in Corporation Road, bringing electricity into town to replace gas lighting. Horse tramways had come to Newport in 1875, but were taken over by the Corporation in 1901. Electricity with overhead electric power wires replaced most horse tramways with electric powered cars, and these were almost all gone by 1903.

WALKING IN BELLE VUE PARK 1932 N25118

Did you know?
Big Freeze
In the winter of 1894 there was an exceptionally deep freeze that lasted for three months. All but the largest of the town water mains were frozen solid and water taps had to be fitted in the streets for the use by ordinary people. Ice in Newport Docks was 6 inches thick.

BELLE VUE PARK 1925 77456

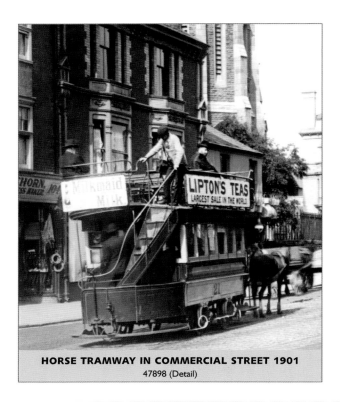

HORSE TRAMWAY IN COMMERCIAL STREET 1901
47898 (Detail)

STREET LIGHT IN COMMERCIAL STREET 1901
47897x (Detail)

ELECTRIC TRAM 1910 62509x (Detail)

John's Directory of Newport for 1927 reported:

'The Electric Tramways consist of some 7.59 route miles, mostly double track, embracing five routes, and there are 58 cars. There are also several Motor Bus routes in operation.'

In 1928 the Corporation started to convert tramcar routes to motorbus routes and by 1936 decided to scrap the remaining routes. The last tram service was withdrawn in September 1937 and a large enthusiastic crowd gathered in the town to see the last tramcar depart for the depot. Souvenir hunters then got busy removing anything they could as a memento. One tram car seat resurfaced a few years ago and was presented to Newport Museum.

BUS ON THE TOWN BRIDGE c1955　N25122 (Detail)

BUS QUEUE IN HIGH STREET c1950　N25140 (Detail)

BUS QUEUE IN HIGH STREET c1950 N25140

BUS ON THE TOWN BRIDGE c1955 N25122

The Transporter Bridge

Parliamentary consent for the construction of the transporter bridge was obtained in 1900, but it took four years to complete in the face of innumerable engineering problems and cost an estimated £98,000.

The latticework steel towers were built on stone piers with steel shoes. To construct the tower bases airtight chamber were constructed under each of the stone piers and pressure in the chambers was maintained at a higher level than outside. Men were sent into the chambers through airlocks to excavate the foundations, and at the end of each day the pressure in the chamber was reduced to allow the pier base to be gradually lowered. It was the first time such a system had been used in Britain and, despite the complicated technology used, not a single life was lost during construction, and the only accidents were minor ones.

Godfrey, Lord Tredegar ceremoniously opened the bridge on 12 September 1906 and, despite a chequered career, it is still in operation today. The span of the bridge between the two towers is 196.6 metres, the height from ground level to the main boom is 73.7 metres, and the gondola can carry up to six cars and twenty foot passengers on each trip. It takes about one and a half minutes to cross the river once the gondola is moving.

Newport Transporter Bridge is the oldest working bridge of its type in the country. The only other working transporter bridge in Britain is at Middlesbrough and was opened in 1911. Fewer than 20 transporter bridges were built worldwide between 1893 and 1916, and only six are thought to still be surviving.

THE TRANSPORTER BRIDGE 1910 62513 (Detail)
Waiting for the gondola.

THE TRANSPORTER BRIDGE 2004 N25714k (Bob Trett)

THE TRANSPORTER BRIDGE 1906 54935

THE TRANSPORTER BRIDGE 2004 ZZZ01420 (Bob Trett)

By 1898 the firm of Lysaghts had acquired 70 acres of land on the east bank of the Usk. Set up by John Lysaght in 1869, the firm had factories in Bristol and elsewhere, where they produced steel sheets and galvanised iron for the construction of cheap buildings in Britain and the Empire. In order to keep up with demand they needed new sheet mills and chose the site at Newport.

The new mills were called the Orb Works and a branch railway line was constructed to the site from the Great Western Railway main line. Lysaghts also built a wharf to transport steel sheet across the Severn to their Bristol works. Large numbers of workers from both the Tawe Valley near Swansea and Wolverhampton, where Lysaghts had works, moved into the area and needed houses, so new streets of houses were built around the present Corporation Road. Other new facilities that were also set up included the Corporation Hotel in 1898, a Working Men's Social Club in 1902, and new churches and schools. in 1928 the Lysaght Institute opened, providing the company's employees with good leisure facilities including a billiard room, a skittle alley, a public bar and a lounge bar.

With all this expansion on the east bank putting increasing pressure on the Town Bridge (next to the Castle), the Corporation decided to build another bridge, close to the docks on the west of the river and to the Orb Steelworks on the east of the river. There was a small ferry service operating here but, with the problems created by tides, it wasn't an option in solving the transport problem. A conventional bridge or a swing bridge was also ruled out because of the width of the river channel and the need to provide clearance for large ships. Even a tunnel was considered, but the cost was thought to be too high.

In the end, Robert Haynes, the Borough Engineer, came up with a solution after he saw another type of bridge, using an aerial ferry, built at Rouen by a French architect called Ferdinand Arnodin. This type of bridge was called a 'transbordeur', which is the origin of the name transporter bridge. A transporter bridge has a ferry (known as a gondola) that is suspended by cables from a moving carriage (known as a traveller) running along a high level beam (known as a boom). The boom is held up on two towers, one on either bank, and carries a rail track on which the moving traveller can be pulled along by cables operated from a motor house. Passengers board the gondola from approach roads under each of the towers and can then be transported to the other side.

NEWPORT BRIDGE c1955 N25228 (Detail)

CYCLIST IN HIGH STREET 1910 62509v (Detail)

In 1913, whilst Newport continued to prosper, Courtney, the new Lord Tredegar, inherited uncle Godfrey's vast wealth. Although still involved with the town, Courtney's main interests were hunting, fishing and shooting, travel and his private yacht 'The Liberty'. His son Evan inherited the title on his death in 1934, but continued to live a lavishly eccentric aristocratic life in London.

Evan was very much a society man. He served in the Welsh Guards during the First World War and then became a shareholder in a restaurant in London. He numbered many of the most famous and talented people of the time among his friends - Somerset Maughan, the heiress Nancy Cunard, Noel Coward, H G Wells, Aldous Huxley and Augustus John to name but a few - and his dinner parties were said to be amongst the most amusing in London.

When he married Lois Sturt, herself a leading society figure, in 1928 the newspapers referred to 'the union of two of the brightest and most original brains in Society'. After the wedding in Brompton, Evan and Lois left for their honeymoon in Evan's own plane from Croydon Airport.

He often spent the weekend at Tredegar House, where he would entertain houseguests, including some notorious ones like the occultist Aleister Crowley. The weekend parties were lavish, as witnessed by one of his guests:

'It started with a five-course dinner being served at 8 pm, but this was frequently late as people were arriving from London by train, where they would be met by two Rolls Royce motorcars flying the Morgan flag on the bonnet. A band or harpist would be hired to play in the entrance hall, and the dinner would be served by the Butler and two or three footmen in livery. After the meal the ladies retired to the New Hall, whilst the gentlemen remained in the dining room, drinking port and liqueurs, and the evening would finish by some guests playing charades and others, bridge'.

One of Evan's greatest eccentricities was his collection of animals. He changed the stables at Tredegar House into a menagerie, but a baboon called Bimbo had the run of the house, where there was also a small alligator, and he kept a fierce white artic owl in his bedroom, boasting that he was the only person that could handle it. There was a macaw called Blue Boy that would climb up his trouser leg and kangaroos and monkeys that were kept outside. On one occasion a black widow spider that was kept in a glass case in the most formal of the staterooms, the Gilt Room, escaped during a party and was eventually found climbing up a curtain.

Evan was the last of the Morgans to live at Tredegar House. He died in 1949 and the title passed to an elderly uncle, who transferred the estates to his son John. Evan's had funded his lifestyle from capital rather than his annual income. This, together with paying off heavy death duties, forced John to sell the house in 1951 when it became a Catholic girls' boarding school. When John died in 1962 without an heir the title died out ending the long link between the Morgans of Tredegar House and Newport.

Though the Morgan's power and influence may have been dissipating, Newport itself was thriving. Its importance as a port

THE ORANGERY GARDEN AT TREDEGAR HOUSE 2004 N25704k (Bob Trett)

was particularly significant during the two World Wars. At the outbreak of the First World War Newport police seized the first ship captured during the hostilites a German merchant ship called the 'Belgia' anchored ten miles from the town - and brought it into Newport Docks.

TREDEGAR HOUSE, THE NORTH-EAST FRONT 2003 N25717k (Bob Trett)

TREDEGAR HOUSE, THE MAIN ENTRANCE 2004
ZZZ01419 (Bob Trett)

Did you know?
Lady Katherine Carnegie

Evan, Lord Tredegar's mother, Lady Katherine Carnegie was the daughter of James, 9th Earl of Southesk and married Courtney Morgan in 1890. She preferred her house in Dorking, Surrey to South Wales where she indulged her curious hobby of making intricate bird nests that she would leave in trees and bushes in the hope that birds would use them. Her eccentricity increased as she grew older until she became convinced that she was herself a bird and would even sit on her own nests. Evan would invite visitors to the house to meet his mother saying: 'She makes the most wonderful nests'.

Did you know?

First World War Losses

During the First World War the vast majority of a total 1,472 Newport men and 4 Newport women who lost their lives perished at the Battle of Ypres on 8 May 1915. That day 1,371 Newport men died.

SOLDIERS IN HIGH STREET 1910   62509v (Detail)

CENOTAPH 1925   77462

During the Second World War Newport was bombed, but not as badly as other towns, such as Swansea. The first attack was on 26 June 1940, when a single bomber dropped a string of bombs on an oil depot. The most serious attack was on houses on the corner of Eveswell Street and Archibald Street when 30 people were killed. In all 51 people died during air attacks on Newport and 63 were seriously injured.

Did you know?
Heinkel Bomber Pilot Capture

On 13 September 1940 a Heinkel bomber was caught by a barrage balloon cable while flying at low altitude above Belle Vue Park. The plane crashed into a house in Stow Park Avenue killing two children. The pilot, Oberleutnant Harry Wappler bailed out and was captured. He was the only survivor of the crew.

Many warships finished up in Newport at the yard of iron merchant, John Cashmore. His main office was in West Bromwich, Birmingham, but before the First World War he had established a ship-breaking yard near Newport's Town Dock and broke many ships, there, including large liners like the Empress of France, which was over 20,000 tons, and the White Star Liner R M S 'Doric'. Built in Belfast, the 'Doric' weighed over 16,000 tons and could carry 2,300 passengers with a crew of 350 and had her maiden voyage in 1923. In 1935 she was badly damaged in collision with a French steamer in fog off Cape Finisterre.

War Heroes

Newport had its fair share of heroes. Commander John Wallace 'Tubby' Linton, who served on the submarine HMS 'Turbulent' in the Mediterranean in 1942-1943, was awarded the Victoria Cross posthumously and is the town's only holder of the award. According to an official notice in the London Gazette, he was responsible for sinking nearly 100,000 tons of enemy shipping, including one cruiser, one destroyer, one U-boat and 28 supply ships. The 'Turbulent' went missing in 1943 and was almost certainly lost in a minefield. Wilbert Widdicombe of Newport was one of two who survived the sinking of the freighter SS 'Anglo-Saxon'. The 'Anglo-Saxon' sailed from Newport on 6 August 1940 and was torpedoed in the Atlantic by a German surface raider, the 'Widder' on the evening of the 21 August. The crew took to the boats but were machine gunned down by the raider. Seven had escaped in the ship's jolly boat, two of them wounded by machine gun fire, and over the next 25 days five more men died. With less than fifteen days provisions, the two survivors Widdicombe and Robert Tapscott of Cardiff drifted across the Atlantic.

After 70 days and 2,700 miles they came ashore on an island in the Bahamas, having survived on rainwater, seaweed and on flying fish. For the last eight days of their journey they'd had no water.

Their survival created great interest and they toured the United States to promote the plight of Britain before the United States had entered the War. Thirteen Newport men were among those who died on the SS 'Anglo-Saxon'. An American museum originally acquired the jolly boat, but it is now on display in the Imperial War Museum in London.

Her passengers were transferred to another ship, but the 'Doric' was badly damaged and sold to John Cashmore for breaking up after only 12 years in service. She caused great interest in Newport when she first arrived and a lunch and charity ball were held on board in aid of the Royal Gwent Hospital and the ship was illuminated at night. There was a major auction of her furnishings and fittings including tables, chairs, brass work and vast numbers of lavatories. Her relics were scattered in buildings throughout Newport and an extremely fine boardroom model is now on display in Newport Museum, along with chairs and other mementos.

Any story of Newport would be incomplete without mention of Super Tramp William Henry Davies. W H Davies was born in 1871 in Portland Street, Pill. Already badly behaved as a teenager, he was birched for shoplifting. When he left school he worked as an ironmonger before becoming an apprentice picture frame maker. But this also didn't suit him and in 1893 he left for the United States and spent the next six years working or begging his way across America until he decided to work his passage back home on cattle ships. Back in Britain he was frequently jailed for vagrancy and lost a leg under the wheels of an express train he tried to board by jumping.

Davies had to return to London where he turned to writing and received much acclaim for his poetry. In 1938 he returned to honours in Newport - the unveiling of a plaque in his honour and an address by the Poet Laureate John Masefield. This was his

last appearance for by now he was unwell and he died in September 1940, aged 69.

Most of his poetry is about nature or life on the road, and he wrote with a natural simple, earthy style. He also wrote two novels and autobiographical works. Today he is best remembered for just two lines from a poem titled 'Leisure':

'What is this life if, full of care,
We have no time to stand and stare?'

BENCH SEAT IN BELLE VUE PARK c1932
N25117c (Detail)

CHILDREN IN BELLE VUE PARK c1932
N25117x (Detail)

SCHOOL ATTENDANCE MEDAL FOR 1904/5
AWARDED TO HYWEL OWEN ZZZ01406
Courtesy of www.newportpast.com

SCHOOL ATTENDANCE MEDAL (REVERSE)
ZZZ01407 Courtesy of www.newportpast.com

In the 1900's schools received grants according to the attendance record of their pupils. To encourage punctuality and to discourage truancy, pupils were given attendance medals; these from the Newport area show Newport Castle on the reverse.

BELLE VUE PARK c1932 N25117

NEWPORT FROM THE AIR 1963 AFA115869

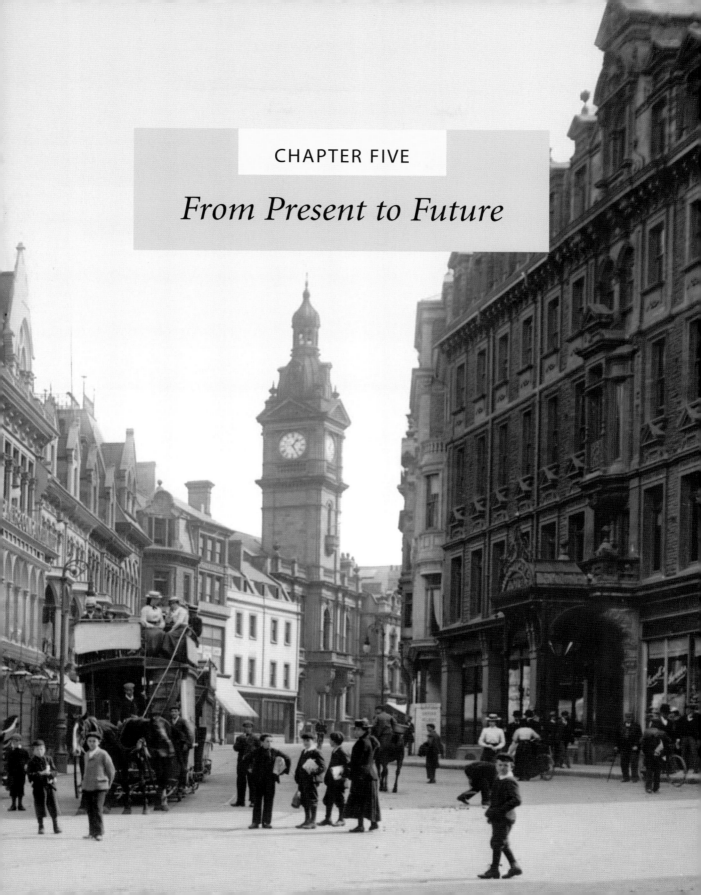

CHAPTER FIVE

From Present to Future

THE DECLINE of the coal and steel industries during the 1930s, and again after the end of the First World War, led to a period of economic depression and high unemployment in Newport. Many years later it was the opening of the giant Spencer Steel Works at Llanwern by Richard, Thomas and Baldwins Ltd that injected a new prosperity into the area.

In the 1980s there were five steelworks in Newport, but as the steel industry began to decline the town needed to diversify. New manufacturing operations included engineering works, an aluminium plant, a chemical works and a number of high technology industries, such as Panasonic.

The Business Statistics Office, providing central government with the majority of its trade and industry statistics, has moved into the town. The Patent Office moved to Newport in 1991, bringing 1000 new jobs, and Newport Passport Office is the regional centre for all of Wales and for much of the South and South West of England.

Llanwern Steel Works

The steel plant was built on a 2,800 acre site, about three and a half miles long, on low lying land on the Gwent Levels to the east of Newport. Nine million tons of shale was needed to build up the site and 93,000 piles were driven into the ground to support the buildings' heavy equipment. It took over three years to construct and was opened by Queen Elizabeth in 1962. It was to employ over 10,000 workers making sheet steel in large quantities, mainly for the car industry. Eventually, though, economic problems forced the plant to slim down until ownership was finally transferred to British Steel, and by the 1980s fewer than 4,500 people were working at Llanwern.

In 1984 Llanwern produced 2.1 million tons of steel (6,000 tons a day). It used 26 thousand tons of coal or coke a week, all of which came from South Wales mines. It used 55 thousand tons of iron ore a week and 8 thousand tons of limestone. It generated its own electricity for the site and still provided 110 megawatts for the national grid. It also used 14 million gallons of water a day to top up the reservoirs containing 250 million gallons of water on site.

In 1999 British Steel merged with the Dutch firm Hoogovens to form the company called Corus and in 2001 the new company announced the closure of steel making at Llanwern, with the direct loss of a further 1,340 jobs.

LLANWERN STEELWORKS 2002
N25705k (Bob Trett)

The works viewed from the top of the Transporter Bridge.

After a chequered history, Newport Docks is still thriving, though. In 1880 two and a half million tons of coal were transported from Newport, but by 1922, when ownership of the docks passed to the Great Western Railway Company, this trade was in steep decline. In 1930 the Town Dock was filled and business was concentrated on the Alexandra North and South Docks. After nationalisation in 1948 the docks came under control of the British Transport Commission and then the British Transport Docks Board and a variety of cargos as well as coal was handled. In 1975 the shipping of iron ore ceased. In December 1982 docks in Britain were denationalised and Associated British Ports took over operation of Newport Docks the following year.

Associated British Ports is today the United Kingdom's largest port operator, and runs 21 ports around the country. Newport Docks are able to handle a wide range of traffic including fresh produce, such as bananas, vehicles, steel, solid fuels, minerals, timber, scrap and general cargo.

There have been dramatic changes to the road system around Newport too. On 8 September 1966 Queen Elizabeth II opened the first Severn Bridge, near Chepstow, to carry the M4 into Wales. This bridge replaced the old ferry service from Aust to Beachley Head and crosses two rivers, the Wye and the Severn, a distance of three miles. The effect on South Wales has been dramatic: in May 1989 a record 76,182 vehicles crossed the bridge in one day. The M4 motorway was extended to Newport between 1966 and 1967

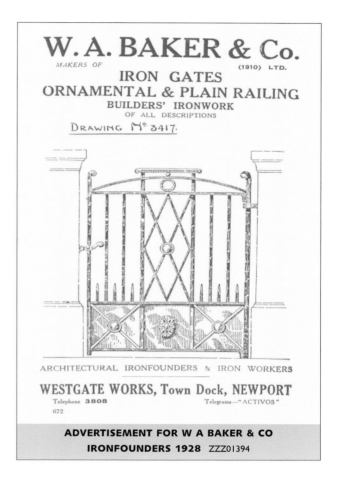

ADVERTISEMENT FOR W A BAKER & CO IRONFOUNDERS 1928 ZZZ01394

and boasts double tunnels through Brynglas Hill at Newport - still a notorious bottleneck for traffic.

The opening of the M4 corridor, first to Newport, then on to Cardiff, Swansea and South West Wales, has brought increased demand for land for new development. Industrial and commercial sites, leisure facilities, new housing and additional roads have all put pressure on the land around Newport. Particularly at risk have been the Gwent Levels, the low-lying area that formed part of the Severn Estuary basin until seawalls were constructed in the Middle Ages. The Levels still retain much of their old character, with historic villages and flat fields surrounded by drainage ditches known as reens but big developments such as the Llanwern Steelworks have taken sizeable chunks of the Levels.

In 1996 the Prince of Wales opened the new bridge for the second Severn crossing, which replaced a section of the M4 motorway and increased the potential for new development in the area.

One controversial proposal in recent years has been for an international airport, built out onto the Severn Estuary near Newport.

Newport has also been involved in the barrage craze. Plans for river barrages are not new: as early as 1840 there were proposals for a barrage across the Severn Estuary. In 1978 a Severn Barrage Committee was set up to advise the Government on 'whether to proceed with a scheme for harnessing the tidal energy of the Severn Estuary'. The Committee spent two years examining the potential for a barrage and concluded that it could be built and the best location would be from Brean Down in Somerset to Lavernock Point in South Glamorgan. Further work was entrusted to the Severn Tidal Power Group, a consortium of construction companies. In 1989 they reported that the scheme would be too costly. Nevertheless, the idea is still being discussed as a future possibility. Needless to say, the effect would be enormous, including land reclamation from the estuary, damage to wildlife - particularly migratory birds - and changes in the tides.

WEST USK LIGHTHOUSE 1910 62517

Newport Borough Council has had its own plans for a barrage. In 1989 they adopted a Riverfront Development Strategy. This involved the construction of a barrage across the River Usk between the George Street and the Transporter bridges, in the vicinity of the former Town Dock. The barrage was intended to provide a constantly higher water level on the river that would submerge the 'visually unattractive' mud-banks, which are exposed at low tide. This, it was claimed, would enhance the appearance of the river through Newport and provide some additional flood protection. The scheme would also encourage investment, including new 'executive' housing, prestige offices and new leisure and tourists facilities. The barrage design included overflow weirs, sluice gates, a fish pass for migratory fish such as salmon, and a lock for small vessels. Later, plans were also drawn up for a road crossing on the barrage. Extensive investigations were undertaken and a detailed planning study produced. The estimated cost of the whole scheme was about £60,000,000.

The plans went to a public inquiry in 1994: there were 36 days sitting and about 16 days of site inspections. Of the 277 objections to the scheme, most concerned harm to the passage of fish. There were also concerns that there might be more flooding, ground instability, silting in the river and the harm to the appearance of the river and townscape of Newport. In 1995 the Secretary of State for Wales turned down the scheme: it was felt that there was not enough of a case for the barrage as an economic catalyst and that there would be irreversible harm to the landscape upstream of the barrage and on the fish population. Newport was told to

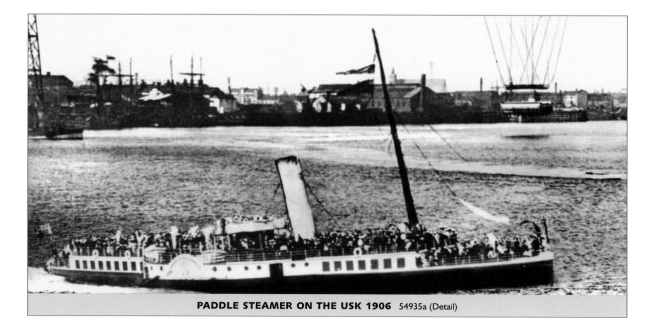

PADDLE STEAMER ON THE USK 1906 54935a (Detail)

regenerate the riverfront in other ways - hopefully this will now include an appreciation of the tidal changes and of the appearance of the mudflats at low tide!

The Cardiff Bay Barrage, however, did happen. Work started in 1994 and was completed in 1999 to create a freshwater inland lake fed by the Rivers Taff and Ely. Whilst some in Newport may have gritted their teeth that the Cardiff Bay Barrage got the green light, the scheme has affected Newport positively. One condition for the barrage to go ahead was the creation of an 'alternative feeding ground' for the thousands of migrating waders and wildfowl that flocked to the tidal mudflats at Cardiff Bay. And so the Gwent Levels Wetland Reserve came into being, with its new salt marshes and saltwater lagoons, reed-beds and lowland wet grasslands in a thousand acres of land between Uskmouth and Goldcliff. Gradually the Reserve is attracting birds such as breeding avocets, bitterns, short-eared owls and large numbers of lapwings and waterfowl.

Plans for Newport's resurgence after the First World War included new buildings and a changed town centre and one of the most impressive of these new buildings is the Civic Centre. Part of the complex including courts was built in 1937-39, but the central entrance and clock tower were built in 1964. Set on a hill site, the Civic Centre's tall and tapering white clock tower dominates the area and can be seen from miles away. Inside there is a square central hall with eleven grand and colourful murals about Newport, painted by the artist Hans Feibusch.

CIVIC CENTRE AND LAW COURTS c1950 N25138 (Detail)

George Street Bridge

The last of Hans Feibusch's murals in the Civic Centre shows the then brand new George Street Bridge. It was Newport's second road bridge and was built between 1962 and 1964 when it was the first cantilever bridge in Britain. Massive cables that pass through the tall concrete masts support the weight of the bridge. This type of construction has since been used successfully elsewhere, including on the second Severn Crossing.

GEORGE STREET BRIDGE c1960 N25251 (Detail)

GEORGE STREET BRIDGE 2004
N25719k (Bob Trett)

The new Southern Distributor Road Bridge can be seen under the George Street Bridge.

SOUTHERN DISTRIBUTOR ROAD BRIDGE, PRIOR TO OPENING IN 2004 N25708k (Bob Trett)
Newport's newest river crossing, serving the Southern Distributor Road.

GEORGE STREET BRIDGE c1960 N25251

NEWPORT CIVIC CENTRE AND CLOCK TOWER 2004
N25706k (Bob Trett)

**NEWPORT FROM BRYNGLAS HILL, SHOWING THE
CIVIC CENTRE TOWER 2004** N25707k (Bob Trett)

FROM THE TOWER OF ST WOOLOS CATHEDRAL c1955 N25240

The new town centre created in the 1960s included an inner ring road (Kingsway), a bus station, multi-storey car parks, shops and offices, a theatre (the Dolmen) and a central square (John Frost Square). In 1968 the Museum and Library complex was opened facing onto John Frost Square. This Museum was only the second purpose built museum to have been built in Britain after the Second World War.

This was also the era of new housing estates, often built on what had been open fields, as neighbourhood units with their own schools, shops, churches, pubs and open spaces. These supplemented the pre-war housing and the small prefabs that had been erected as emergency post-war houses in 1946 and 1947. One of the largest was the Duffryn Estate, built in a wooded area close to Tredegar House, where two-storey houses were grouped around grassy courts and play areas to create a village feeling, well away from through road traffic.

By the end of the 1960s Newport Council controlled about 15,000 dwellings spread throughout the Borough. But, as with some of the flat-roofed office blocks and public buildings, the new estates were not universally successful in improving the quality of life of the people. Old areas like Pill declined, whilst some of the new green-field developments lacked community spirit and felt isolated. Fortunately high-rise towers were not a dominant feature of the new estates, and some of the worst have now been demolished. More recently new housing associations have taken over control from the local authority and areas like Pill have seen fresh investment.

Spiritually, with its mixed ethnic community, Newport has a wide range of churches, chapels, mosques, meeting houses and halls for all religions. In 1921, with the dis-establishment of the Church in Wales, the Diocese of Monmouth was created out of the Diocese of Llandaff. St Woolos, the medieval parish of Newport, was declared its Pro-Cathedral. The town's prestige was enhanced when St Woolos was granted full Cathedral status in 1949. Between 1961 and 1962 a new chancel was built to replace the Victorian one. This features the work of the artist John Piper: a large abstract mural and window behind the high altar. Elsewhere in Newport churches and chapels have been restored or converted to other uses, a few have been demolished and one, the Wesleyan Methodist Chapel in Commercial Road, has been converted to a mosque.

Did you know?
Population Figures

The 2001 census showed that Newport had a resident population of 137,011. This was an increase of 2.8% over the population in 1991, and compared with an average increase of 4.3% for this period in England and Wales. 70.5% of males aged 16 to 74 were 'economically active' (i.e. employed), but this had declined from 74.4% in 1991. The female 'economic activity' rate was 56.1%, showing an increase from 52.1% in 1991. In 2001 the City of Newport had 56,535 households with residents, an increase of 7.6% since 1991.

Though artistic life in Newport has always flourished, until the 1990s there was little in the way of street sculpture. Except for a statue to Sir Charles Morgan, originally unveiled in 1948 and re-sited in 1992, there was only a metal sculpture by the artist Harvey Hood called Arch Form, erected in 1981 and standing outside the Railway Station.

More entertaining are the tile mosaics by the artist Kenneth Budd. His 1978 mosaic mural of the Chartists at the entrance to John Frost Square attracts great interest. Other Budd mosaics include murals depicting stallholders near the Provisions Market, and another mural representing the canal and the railway near Newport Castle.

By the 1990s a new wave of sculptures had started to appear in the streets and open spaces of Newport. In 1989 an elaborate bronze sculpture entitled Unity, Prudence, Energy by artist Christopher Kelly was unveiled outside the Westgate Hotel: its intention was to symbolise the three Chartist ideals. Another bronze sculpture by Paul Kinkaid was commissioned in 1990 and stands in Commercial Street. It depicts a shrouded figure to commemorate super-tramp poet W H Davies.

By far the most numerous of the new sculptures are by the artist Sebastian Boyeson. These include a memorial to the merchant navy, with a seated figure of Navigation on a tall column, set up at the south end of Commercial Street in 1991. His sculpture This Little Piggy, of a pig with a basket of fruit and vegetables strapped to its back, was unveiled outside the provisions market in 1994. The Bell Carrier, a life-size bronze bull bearing a bell and bell frame on its back and representing the legend of the founding of St Woolos Church, was unveiled at the entrance to John Frost Square in 1995.

THE BELL CARRIER 2004 N25709k (Bob Trett)

One of Newport's many sculptures by Sebastian Boyeson.

Town Sculpture

The most bizarre piece of new public art, designed and made by Andy Plant, is an automaton clock in the form of an arch, entitled In the Nick of Time. In 1992 it was Newport's contribution to the Ebbw Vale Garden Festival and was re-erected in John Frost Square after the Festival. On the hour the structure opens up, showing a devil, then skeletons, then figures of workmen mending the clock, followed by a cuckoo and bells. It has been described as 'a cross between a cuckoo clock and an espresso machine'.

Steel Wave by Peter Fink, by far the largest sculpture in Newport, is on the riverfront. It is a huge scarlet steel structure with two vaulted struts supporting a hoop and was set up in 1990 as a tribute to both Newport's steelworkers and seafarers. It has been Newport's most controversial work of art, admired by some but felt by others to be a monstrous blot on the landscape. Whatever the reaction it has become, along with the Transporter Bridge, one of the leading symbols of the City.

IN THE NICK OF TIME 2004
N25710k (Bob Trett)

'A cross between a cuckoo clock and an espresso machine … the only white knuckle clock in the world'.

In the background is the provisions market.

STEEL WAVE 2004
N25712k (Bob Trett)

In the 1974 local government reorganisation the historic County of Monmouthshire made way for Gwent County Council, and Newport Borough incorporated neighbouring rural districts, including the historic town of Caerleon. Gwent County Council itself was swept aside in 1996 and a new Newport County Borough Council gained more powers and more responsibilities. The final accolade came in 2002 when the Borough was awarded city status in celebration of the Queen's Golden Jubilee.

A few years earlier, in 1999 the town's status had already been raised, when it gained a university, the University of Wales College Newport (previously Gwent College of Higher Education, based in Clarence Place and Allt-yr-yn Avenue Newport, and in College Crescent Caerleon). The University offered courses leading to honours degrees and other professional qualifications in art and design, education, science and technology. Newport's new status as a city allowed the University to expand, especially at the Caerleon campus, although the Clarence Place College has now been vacated. On 21 April 2004 the University was designated the University of Wales, Newport and in a speech that year the Vice-Chancellor claimed the University to be a 'big-ticket item' in regard to the City's economy. The University does indeed turn over around £30 million per annum, employs between 800 and 900 people and attracts students from all over the United Kingdom and overseas.

Newport still has its ups and downs. The unemployment rate for Newport is below the average rate for England and Wales. In 1996 there was the good news that Newport had won a battle for a 6,000-job factory on the outskirts of the town. The Korean company LG announced a £1.7 billion investment that would include one factory making TV components and another making silicon chips. The deal included land and financial incentives from the Welsh Development Agency and Newport County Borough Council. LG, formerly known as Lucky Goldstar, was the biggest company of its type in Korea and the news seemed a tremendous boost to Newport's economy and prosperity. Unfortunately the dream never materialised. The silicon chip factory remained empty and in May 2003 it was announced that the TV components factory would close down with the loss of almost 900 jobs. On the other hand, there are plans for new schemes, including redevelopment of the town centre and the Llanwern steel-works site.

Newport has always had a strong sporting tradition. Newport Rugby Football Club has a long and distinguished history with the added kudos of being the only team to beat New Zealand's All Blacks during their 1963 - 64 tour. In 2003 the Club merged with Ebbw Vale to become Gwent Dragons at first, and later Newport Gwent Dragons. Their home ground is still Rodney Parade, Newport.

Newport County Football Club was established in 1912 and played at Somerton Park. The Club's fortunes have fluctuated over the years. In 1980 it was promoted to Division 3 and in 1981 it reached the quarter final of the European Cup Winners Cup. But

Did you know?

Newport Boxers

Johnny Basham of Newport became British Welterweight Boxing Champion in 1914, when he defeated the reigning champion Johnny Summers. He held the title until June 1920. In 1983 David Pearce of Newport became British Heavyweight Champion, but had to give the title up in 1985 on medical grounds.

name to Newport County A F C and has a new home in the Newport Stadium. Speedway is also very popular in Newport, where the home team is Newport Wasps.

Sports facilities in Newport have developed tremendously in recent years. Among the most recent attractions has been the opening of the Wales National Velodrome, able to host international and national cycling events.

Golf has also taken on an important role in Newport. In 2010 Newport will host the Ryder Cup, when leading golfers from Europe and the USA will battle it out for this prestigious trophy.

It is estimated that 35,000 visitors a day will come to watch play at the Celtic Manor Resort, where a new course is being built to meet international specifications.

in 1989 it was wound up and a new club, Newport A F C was formed to replace it. This became known as the Exiles as the team was forced to play its home games in England for a time. Since then the Club has changed its

THE CELTIC MANOR HOTEL 2004 N25712k (Bob Trett)

Home to the 2010 Ryder Cup.

Newport is a city where the old meets the new. The Transporter Bridge has been renovated and was reopened in 1995. Much of Tredegar House has been carefully restored and, when it was opened to the public in 1974, it was claimed to be the 'finest country house in Wales'. Buildings in Belle Vue Park are about to be restored. The Newport Medieval Ship (earlier and more complete than the Mary Rose in Portsmouth) is undergoing a long conservation programme prior to being displayed in Newport. In the meantime the Riverfront Theatre has been built on the site where it was found and will have a display dedicated to the ship. The city has much to be proud of in its past and much to look forward to in its future.

NEWPORT AT NIGHT FROM THE RIVER 2004 N25718k (Bob Trett)

ACKNOWLEDGEMENTS

I am grateful to the following for their assistance and support with this book. Ray Howell of the University of Wales, Newport; Victoria Newton Davies and Rachael Anderton of Newport Museum and Art Gallery; Newport Reference Library; Gwent Record Office; Anne Leaver and Owain Roberts for the illustration of the Newport Medieval Ship; www.newportpast.com for assistance with illustrations; Roger James for all types of help; Charles Ferris for just being there; and many others for advice and information. I give my special thanks to Frances for suffering all my agonies over a number of months and to whom this book is dedicated.

SELECT BIBLIOGRAPHY

Many of these sources will contain contradictory or inaccurate information. In this book I have tried to obtain the most modern interpretation, based as far as possible on original sources. This is not always possible and inevitably any account of Newport will depend on the accuracy of earlier authors. For other references contact the Newport Reference Library in John Frost Square, Newport.

Anderton, Rachel	Newport East of the River 2002
Bradney, Joseph	A History of Monmouthshire
	Volume V. The Hundred of Newport
	Edited by Madeleine Gray 1993
Coxe, William	An Historical Tour of Monmouthshire 1801
Davies, W H	Autobiography of a Super Tramp 1908
Davis, Haydn	The History of the Borough of Newport 1998
Dawson, Alex	Newport West of the River 1995
Dawson, James W	Commerce and Customs. A History of the Ports of Newport and Caerleon 1932
Freeman, David	Tredegar House (Newport Borough Council Guide) 1982
Griffiths, R A (editor)	Boroughs of Medieval Wales 1978
Howell, Raymond	A History of Gwent 1988
Hildred, Falcon D	Newport Transporter Bridge 1996
Jones, Brynmor Pierce	The Government of Newport (Mon) 1550 - 1850. 1957
Jones, David J V	The Last Rising
	The Newport Chartist Insurrection of 1839 1990
Knight, Cliff V	Pillgwenlly : Newport 1983
Knight, Jeremy K	Caerleon Roman Fortress (Cadw guide) 1988
Newman, John	The Buildings of Wales - Gwent / Monmouthshire 2000
Matthews, J H	Historic Newport 1910
Rees, William	The Charters of the Borough of Newport 1951
Reeves, A C	Newport Lordship 1317 - 1536 1979
Roderick, Alan	The Pubs of Newport 1997
Thomas, D B	Newport Transport : A Brief History 2001
Trett, Bob	Newport Transporter Bridge (Newport Borough Council leaflet) 2001
Wilson, John	Art and Society in Newport : James Flewitt Mullock and the Victorian Achievement 1993

Other authors of useful books and articles on Newport include Terry Underwood, Fred Hando, Chris Barber, John O'Sullivan, Richard Frame and Mike Buckingham. Useful periodicals include the Monmouthshire Antiquary, Gwent Local History, Archaeology in Wales, and Newport Year Books. There are numerous directories, town guides and newspapers. The South Wales Argus has an online archive on www.thisisgwent.co.uk. www.newportpast.com has a detailed account of 19th-century Newport by Derrick Cyril Vaughan. Newport City Council website is www.newport.gov.uk. The Friends of the Newport Medieval Ship have a detailed website on www.thenewportship.com.

Ottakar's Bookshops

Ottakar's bookshops, the first of which opened in Brighton in 1988, can now be found in over 120 towns and cities across the United Kingdom. Expansion was gradual throughout the 1990s, but the chain has expanded rapidly in recent years, with many new shop openings and the acquisition of shops from James Thin and Hammicks.

Ottakar's has always known that a shop's local profile is as important, if not more important, than the chain's national profile, and has encouraged its staff to make their shops a part of the local community, tailoring stock to suit the area and forging links with local schools and businesses.

With a reputation for friendly, intelligent and enthusiastic booksellers, warm, inviting shops with an excellent range of books and related products, Ottakar's is now one of the UK's most popular booksellers. In 2003 and then again in 2004 it won the prestigious Best Bookselling Company of the Year Award at the British Book Awards.

Ottakar's has commissioned The Francis Frith Collection to create a series of town history books similar to this volume, as well as a range of stylish, contemporary localised stationery, including address books, notebooks, day books, and other gift products, all illustrated with historical photographs from the Frith archive.

Participating Ottakar's bookshops can be found in the following towns and cities:

Andover	Eastbourne	Poole
Ashford	Farnham	Redhill
Banbury	Folkestone	Salisbury
Barnstaple	Gloucester	St Albans
Bishop's Stortford	Grimsby	Staines
Brentwood	Guildford	Stevenage
Bromley	Harrogate	Tenterden
Bury St Edmunds	Hastings	Tiverton
Camberley	Horsham	Trowbridge
Carmarthen	King's Lynn	Truro
Cheltenham	Lancaster	Tunbridge Wells
Cirencester	Lincoln	Wells
Coventry	Llandudno	Weston-super-Mare
Crawley	Maidenhead	Windsor
Darlington	Market Harborough	Witney
Dorchester	Newport	Woking
Douglas, Isle of Man	Newton Abbot	Worcester
East Grinstead	Norwich	Yeovil

Francis Frith
Pioneer Victorian Photographer

Francis Frith, founder of the world-famous photographic archive, was a multi-talented man. A devout Quaker and a highly successful Victorian businessman, he was philosophical by nature and pioneering in outlook. By 1855 he had already established a wholesale grocery business in Liverpool, and sold it for the astonishing sum of £200,000, which is the equivalent today of over £15,000,000. Now in his thirties, and captivated by the new science of photography, Frith set out on a series of pioneering journeys up the Nile and to the Near East.

He was the first photographer to venture beyond the sixth cataract of the Nile. Africa was still the mysterious 'Dark Continent', and Stanley and Livingstone's historic meeting was a decade into the future. The conditions for picture taking confound belief. He laboured for hours in his wicker dark-room in the sweltering heat of the desert, while the volatile chemicals fizzed dangerously in their trays. Back in London he exhibited his photographs and was 'rapturously cheered' by members of the Royal Society. His reputation as a photographer was made overnight.

By the 1870s the railways had threaded their way across the country, and Bank Holidays and half-day Saturdays had been made obligatory by Act of Parliament. All of a sudden the working man and his family were able to enjoy days out, take holidays, and see a little more of the world.

With typical business acumen, Francis Frith foresaw that these new tourists would enjoy having souvenirs to commemorate their days out. For the next thirty years he travelled the country by train and by pony and trap, producing fine photographs of seaside resorts and beauty spots that were keenly bought by millions of Victorians. These prints were painstakingly pasted into family albums and pored over during the dark nights of winter, rekindling precious memories of summer excursions. Frith's studio was soon supplying retail shops all over the country, and by 1890 F Frith & Co had become the greatest specialist photographic publishing company in the world, with over 2,000 sales outlets, and pioneered the picture postcard.

Francis Frith had died in 1898 at his villa in Cannes, his great project still growing. By 1970 the archive he created contained over a third of a million pictures showing 7,000 British towns and villages.

Frith's legacy to us today is of immense significance and value, for the magnificent archive of evocative photographs he created provides a unique record of change in the cities, towns and villages throughout Britain over a century and more. Frith and his fellow studio photographers revisited locations many times down the years to update their views, compiling for us an enthralling and colourful pageant of British life and character.

We are fortunate that Frith was dedicated to recording the minutiae of everyday life. For it is this sheer wealth of visual data, the painstaking chronicle of changes in dress, transport, street layouts, buildings, housing and landscape that captivates us so much today, offering us a powerful link with the past and with the lives of our ancestors.

Computers have now made it possible for Frith's many thousands of images to be accessed almost instantly. The archive offers every one of us an opportunity to examine the places where we and our families have lived and worked down the years. Its images, depicting our shared past, are now bringing pleasure and enlightenment to millions around the world a century and more after his death. For further information visit: www.francisfrith.co.uk

FREE PRINT OF YOUR CHOICE

Mounted Print
Overall size 14 x 11 inches (355 x 280mm)

Choose any Frith photograph in this book.
Simply complete the Voucher opposite and return it with your remittance for £2.25 (to cover postage and handling) and we will print the photograph of your choice in SEPIA (size 11 x 8 inches) and supply it in a cream mount with a burgundy rule line (overall size 14 x 11 inches).
Please note: photographs with a reference number starting with a "Z" are not Frith photographs and cannot be supplied under this offer.
Offer valid for delivery to UK addresses only.

PLUS: **Order additional Mounted Prints at HALF PRICE - £7.49 each** (normally £14.99)
If you would like to order more Frith prints from this book, possibly as gifts for friends and family, you can buy them at half price (with no additional postage and handling costs).

PLUS: **Have your Mounted Prints framed**
For an extra £14.95 per print you can have your mounted print(s) framed in an elegant polished wood and gilt moulding, overall size 16 x 13 inches (no additional postage and handling required).

IMPORTANT!

These special prices are only available if you use this form to order . You must use the ORIGINAL VOUCHER on this page (no copies permitted). We can only despatch to one address. This offer cannot be combined with any other offer.

Send completed Voucher form to:
The Francis Frith Collection, Frith's Barn, Teffont, Salisbury, Wiltshire SP3 5QP

CHOOSE A PHOTOGRAPH FROM THIS BOOK

Voucher for **FREE** and Reduced Price Frith Prints

Please do not photocopy this voucher. Only the original is valid, so please fill it in, cut it out and return it to us with your order.

Picture ref no	Page no	Qty	Mounted @ £7.49	Framed + £14.95	Total Cost
		1	Free of charge*	£	£
			£7.49	£	£
			£7.49	£	£
			£7.49	£	£
			£7.49	£	£
			£7.49	£	£

Please allow 28 days for delivery

* Post & handling (UK)	£2.25
Total Order Cost	£

Title of this book . . . .
I enclose a cheque/postal order for £ . . . .
made payable to 'The Francis Frith Collection'

OR please debit my Mastercard / Visa / Switch (Maestro) /Amex card
(credit cards please on all overseas orders), details below

Card Number

Issue No (Switch only)   Valid from (Amex/Switch)

Expires   Signature

Name Mr/Mrs/Ms . . . .
Address . . . .
. . . .
. . . .
. . . . Postcode . . . .
Daytime Tel No . . . .
Email . . . .

Valid to 31/12/07